The Four-Blocks® Literacy Model

The Administrator's Guide to Building Blocks™

by
**Dorothy P. Hall,
Amanda B. Arens,
and
Karen L. Loman**

Carson-Dellosa Publishing Company, Inc.
Greensboro, North Carolina

Dedication

My two coauthors are the daughters of two administrators. I think sometimes the "teaching gene" is passed along. I thought it only fitting that this book be dedicated to these two administrators.

—Dottie Hall

To Amanda's mother, **Sandy Newcomer**:

Your five years as an excellent administrator, and sixteen years as an outstanding teacher, were outdone only by your thirty plus years of motherhood. Your dedication to education in the state of Missouri was well known by all with whom you worked. Your dedication to your daughters continues to affect us each day. Your love for teaching and your love for the written word have been passed on, and for that I am grateful. I only wish you were still here to share this exciting moment with me. So, this book is dedicated to you, Mother. I miss you and I love you.

—Amanda Arens

To Karen's dad, **Dr. Keith Bench**:

An exceptional school administrator, my role model for leadership, wisdom, determination, and empathy. Thank you, and Mom, for all of your love, support, and encouragement.

—Karen Loman

Credits

Editor:
Joey Bland

Cover Design:
Annette Hollister-Papp

Layout Design:
Joey Bland

ISBN 0-88724-812-8

Foreword

As I worked with kindergarten teachers to implement the Building-Blocks™ model (Cunningham & Hall, 1996; Hall & Cunningham, 1997; Hall & Williams, 2000) administrators, especially principals who work with and watch teachers daily, asked for checklists to insure that kindergarten teachers were implementing the model correctly. Principals wanted to be sure they knew what to look for in kindergarten lessons so that they could evaluate teachers accurately and plan for staff development when needed. Being busier than I wanted, or needed, to be I just dismissed the thought at first. When this question continued, I knew it was a project that needed to be done.

In the spring of 2001, Amanda Arens and Karen Loman, two wonderful Four-Blocks/Building-Blocks trainers from Missouri, were working with kindergarten teachers and administrators and discussed this project with me. It was then that I decided the book could and would be written—with their help. In the summer of 2001, we wrote the lists and the following fall, administrators and kindergarten teachers used these lists and helped us fine-tune them.

This guide is the result of Amanda and Karen's tireless efforts, along with the principals and teachers they have worked with—especially Terry Frazee and the teachers at Hallsville Elementary in Hallsville, Missouri. I am indebted to Amanda and Karen for their help, both in the initial work of writing these checklists and also for following through and seeing that administrators and teachers found the checklists helpful and useful before we published this work. Pat Cunningham and I have been fortunate to find a whole new "family" with Four Blocks. We have met many wonderful teachers who are now helping us to help other teachers. Thank you Amanda and Karen for everything!

Dottie Hall

Table of Contents

Table of Contents

Introduction

Building Blocks™ is the kindergarten program for the Four-Blocks® Literacy Model. Building Blocks is actually older than Four Blocks. It began over twenty-five years ago when Dr. Patricia Cunningham talked to her graduate students about developmentally appropriate reading and writing practices, and Elaine Williams, a kindergarten teacher and graduate student, began doing these activities in her classroom. Elaine was teaching just outside of Winston-Salem, North Carolina in a rural community. The city/county school system bused students from the inner-city neighborhoods to schools surrounding the city to achieve court-ordered racial balance. Elaine found, like many other kindergarten teachers, that the activities she learned from Pat Cunningham at Wake Forest University worked for all of her students. Elaine also learned that you did not have to use traditional first-grade activities in kindergarten in order to teach all children to read and write.

With the success of Four Blocks (Cunningham, Hall, and Defee, 1991; 1998) in the 1990s, administrators in some schools and school systems began to ask, "Why not just begin Four Blocks in kindergarten?" Pat Cunningham and Dottie Hall, originators of the Four-Blocks® Model, quickly said, "No, there are more appropriate activities for kindergarten!" These kindergarten-appropriate activities were put together and called "Building Blocks" because Pat Cunningham and Dottie Hall knew young children needed these "blocks" to build upon if they were to be successful in first grade. Cunningham and Hall then started talking and writing about the "Building-Blocks" framework—activities especially for kindergarten students.

Why an Administrator's Guide to Building Blocks?

This book is meant to serve as a valuable resource for both administrators and kindergarten teachers who want to implement Building Blocks in kindergarten and make sure that this model is done correctly. We hope that administrators, especially those responsible for seeing that kindergarten teachers implement the model correctly, will find it a valuable tool to better understand the Building-Blocks™ Literacy Model, evaluate kindergarten teachers, and plan for staff development when needed. Our goal is to help administrators know what to look for when they observe kindergarten teachers doing Building-Blocks lessons. They can also use these checklists as the basis of follow-up discussions with kindergarten teachers after watching a Building-Blocks lesson.

How Can Teachers Use These Checklists?

This guide is also a resource for teachers who, after reading *Month-by-Month Reading and Writing in Kindergarten* (Hall and Cunningham, 1997) and *The Teacher's Guide to Building Blocks™* (Hall and Williams, 2000), want checklists to see if they are implementing Building-Blocks activities correctly. These checklists can be used for self-assessment; it is our hope that they will help kindergarten teachers know what they are doing right, what they could improve, and what they are not doing and should be doing.

Planning Staff Development for Kindergarten Teachers

There are a number of ways for kindergarten teachers to become familiar with the Building-Blocks™ Model. The most popular way is attending a Building-Blocks workshop or seminar in your area or a Four-Blocks/Building-Blocks conference in North Carolina. Some schools and school systems hire a presenter and provide a workshop for all their kindergarten teachers. In doing so, they see that every teacher gets the same experience; but some "trainers" or presenters are better than others. While some presenters claim to be "trainers" because they have attended one or two Building-Blocks sessions, they have not had enough experience with the model to help others. Others claim to be trained and do not present the model correctly to teachers and administrators, and thus confuse more than help teachers. So buyers beware! There is no "train the trainer" model for Four Blocks or Building Blocks, nor are there any "certified" trainers for Four Blocks or Building Blocks. There are many wonderful teachers, former teachers, and former administrators who offer this training, though. A list can be found on the Four-Blocks Web site at *www.wfu.edu/~cunningh/fourblocks*. True Four-Blocks trainers do not "in-service" kindergarten teachers with other grade levels because "one size fits all" does not work when talking about the two models.

Others ways that kindergarten teachers learn about the model are by reading *The Teacher's Guide to Building Blocks™* and *Month-by-Month Reading and Writing for Kindergarten*, and discussing these ideas and activities with one another, a seasoned Building-Blocks teacher, or on the Building-Blocks mailring at *www.teachers.net*.

How much training a teacher needs depends upon the teacher, his or her knowledge of early reading and writing practices, and the teacher's past experiences. Extensive training is not necessary for many kindergarten teachers who have kept up with the latest research and methods. Many teachers learn as they teach, and the two basic books listed above can provide ongoing support. When a teacher wants more knowledge on a topic, staff development can and should be provided. Often schools or school systems have teachers who can provide this help or staff development locally. If not, a presenter can usually be found and hired by a school, two or more schools training together, or a school system.

Introducing teachers to the model is just the beginning. Kindergarten teachers need ongoing support. Administrators can take advantage of weekly grade-level meetings before, during, or after school to provide staff development for kindergarten teachers who want help, or feel there is an activity they want to know more about.

There are many ways to help kindergarten teachers.

1. The first, and probably the best thing administrators can do is to affirm what kindergarten teachers do well—and every teacher has some strengths.

2. The second way to help kindergarten teachers is to have staff development that is just for them. When talking about reading and writing in kindergarten, there is no reason why teachers at any other grade level (except maybe first-grade teachers) should be there.

3. The third way to help is by letting teachers visit kindergarten classes at a model school (make sure it is a classroom that is worth seeing; a school that follows the Building-Blocks™ Model as intended by the originators and has not strayed!)

4. A fourth way is to have group discussions around a topic ("Morning Message," "Predictable Charts," or any other Building-Blocks activity.)

Besides learning the basic model for Building Blocks, schools have found it useful to include some of the following topics in further staff development.

- Choosing appropriate books to read aloud to kindergarten or primary students

- Choosing appropriate big books for Guided Reading lessons (which include shared, echo, and choral reading)

- Planning Guided Reading lessons with appropriate before, during, and after reading activities

- Using effective reading conference techniques when working with children who are reading and pretend reading in kindergarten

- Documenting students' reading performance through anecdotal note taking

- Administering running records, DRA, IRI, or other reading assessment

- Understanding Gentry's stages of writing/spelling development (Gentry, 1985; Gentry and Gillet, 1993)

- Coaching writing during the writing conference

- Developing appropriate mini-lessons to do before students write

- Providing ways to share kindergarten writing

- Providing a print-rich environment (what to put up in kindergarten classrooms)

- Learning high-frequency words in kindergarten

- Using topics and themes appropriate for kindergarten

- Reading and Writing (Literacy) Centers in kindergarten

How Can Administrators Facilitate and Support Implementation of the Building-Blocks™ Model?

Too often, schools build their staff development for the year around a laundry list of topics, ideas, and programs. Teachers can become overwhelmed if asked to implement too much at one time—especially kindergarten teachers. For successful implementation of the Building-Blocks™ Model, teachers need to remain focused on various aspects of the model. Other areas of the curriculum are not likely to be slighted; usually teachers and administrators find that the good instructional practices learned through this model transfer into other content areas to improve teaching and learning as well. The model will require that teachers and administrators grow together professionally through the process of studying and absorbing the philosophy that drives the model, through the coaching and practicing that occurs, and through discussions and planning with support personnel at school, and between and among schools.

Here are some tips for administrators:

- **Be an active participant in the staff development.** Some teachers say that they know which staff development is truly valued by whether or not the principal attends and participates alongside the faculty. Administrators who understand the Building-Blocks™ Model are able to support it in the classroom by giving constructive feedback.

- **Plan a budget that includes the materials and equipment for success in each classroom.** Teachers need certain basic materials before they can implement the model. Be resourceful in getting what kindergarten teachers need.

- **Observe regularly in classes and offer feedback to all teachers.** Regular observation and constructive feedback will communicate expectations for getting the model implemented and strengthened. An observation checklist for each of the activities is included in this book. Administrators, even those without a strong background in the primary language arts, will find these checklists to be an easy way to give feedback that should strengthen the model. Also, giving feedback on lesson plans can be helpful, especially as teachers begin to implement the model with all its activities.

- **Facilitate networks of support for your faculty.** Because there is much to know about the Building-Blocks™ Model and because the activities change as the curriculum changes throughout the year, teachers need networks of support to rely upon to answer the questions they will have at different points. Principals can encourage kindergarten teachers to plan and discuss these activities together. Additionally, having teachers at a partner school with whom your teachers can communicate about successes and failures can be a real asset.

- **Plan the school schedule to accommodate the model.** Most of the time kindergarten teachers can fit these activities into their daily schedules. They decide what works best at what time, which activities should be done first, and which activities can be done later in the day. Sometimes schedules are obstacles to the success of the Building-Blocks™ Model, especially when there are many interruptions in the class schedule. Teachers need time for these activities, and having a schedule that enables teachers uninterrupted blocks of time allows them to plan a schedule that incorporates the activities on a daily basis.

What is a "Developmentally Appropriate" Kindergarten?

A developmentally appropriate kindergarten is like a good home, where children can learn through playing, cooking, watching, listening, acting, reading or pretend reading, and writing or pretend writing. It is a place where young children can explore their environment, ask questions, and answer questions. It is a place where the teacher is like a good parent—reading to the children and talking about the stories they read; writing for children and allowing them to write for different purposes; taking time with the children to explore their community on field trips; and talking about those experiences together. It is a place where children clean up after themselves, learn more about what interests them most—themselves. Most importantly, it is a place where children learn that reading provides both enjoyment and information, and they develop the desire to learn to read and write (Hall and Cunningham, 1997).

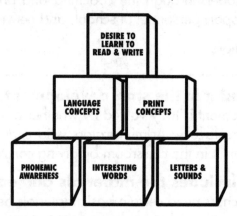

What are the "Building Blocks"?

Recent findings from emergent literacy research have demonstrated that children who easily learn to read and write have a variety of experiences with reading and writing that enable them to profit from school literacy experiences (Cunningham & Allington, 1998). In kindergarten classrooms, teachers can provide a variety of reading and writing experiences from which all children can develop these six critical understandings, which are the "building blocks" of their success.

- Children learn that reading provides both enjoyment and information, and they develop a desire to learn to read and write.

- Students also learn many new concepts and add words and meaning to their speaking vocabularies.

- Children learn print concepts, including how to read from left to write, how to read from top to bottom, etc.

- Children develop phonemic awareness, including the concept of rhyme.

- Students learn to read and write some interesting-to-them words, such as "Pizza Hut®," "cat," and "bear."

- Students learn some letters and sounds—usually connected to the interesting words they have learned.

What Activities Build These Blocks?

Children who come to school reading, or ready to read, have had some reading and writing experiences that help them profit from school instruction. Some children come to school lacking the skills and understanding that lead to success in beginning reading instruction. What can we do to help these children? Kindergarten teachers can provide the necessary experiences for all their students by:

- Reading *to* children (both fiction and nonfiction).

- Reading *with* children (shared reading of predictable books and interactive charts).

- Providing opportunities for children to read *by themselves.*

- Writing *for* children (a Morning Message at the start of the day).

- Writing *with* children (predictable charts and interactive Morning Messages).

- Providing opportunities for children to write *by themselves.*

- Developing phonemic awareness (the oral).

- Working with letters and sounds or phonics (the written).

- Learning some "interesting-to-them" words (names, environmental print, etc.).

These activities are the basis of the Building-Blocks™ Model. (See *Month-by-Month Reading and Writing for Kindergarten* by Hall and Cunningham and *The Teacher's Guide to Building Blocks™* by Hall and Williams for a detailed description of Building Blocks.)

What Does a Building-Blocks Classroom Look Like?

As you look into the classroom, you are likely to see . . .

- Desks or tables arranged in groups of four or six.

- An alphabet stretching across the front of the room, probably above the chalkboard or white board, where young students can easily see it.

- A large colorful calendar, usually on a bulletin board.

- Centers—appropriate centers—placed in and around the room to be used daily at "Center Time."

- Student's names (put up one at a time) displayed under the corresponding letter of the alphabet.

- A pocket chart readily available for a number of activities, such as calendar sentences, names activities, matching sentences, interactive and predictable charts, shared reading activities, etc.

- Students' work and predictable charts displayed in the room, big books made by the class from predictable charts placed in the Reading Center.

- A "Reading Center" with books, books, and more books. During the last half of the year, some books may be placed in baskets and set on the tables for a brief "self-selected reading" time.

- Samples of environmental print (cereal boxes, signs, and packages) placed where students can see and "read" them—usually on a bulletin board.

- A print-rich environment with color words, number words, and theme words displayed.

- A "Writing Center" with writing materials: paper in various colors, sizes, and weights; glue; crayons; markers; pens; pencils; and perhaps a computer.

- Charts of pictures and words displayed on the walls or pictures and words in the "Writing Center" for children to copy, put in books, and read.

- A carpeted area or rug where students gather close to the teacher for "Big Group," teacher read-alouds, shared reading, and to watch the teacher model writing on a board, wall, or chart during the Morning Message, predictable charts, and mini-lessons.

- Math manipulatives and materials for hands-on science activities.

- Teachers and students engaged in teaching and learning!

Administrator's Observation Checklists Early in the Year

A few words of caution about the use of the following pages...

The checklists offered in this book are intended to convey the basics of the Building-Blocks™ Literacy Model for kindergarten. The model is not rigidly defined, especially as teachers gain confidence in the delivery and begin to interject more of their own personalities and creativity. However, some elements define the model, provide the careful balance, are multilevel, and ensure a greater level of success. These checklists are offered in response to administrators and teachers who have asked for more specific details in an attempt to do a better job of getting the Building-Blocks™ Model started.

Also, when the checklists mention that "the lesson lasts as long as the children," it is a reference to ending the lesson when the children are no longer engaged in learning.

Reading to Children

What is reading to children?

Reading to children is when a teacher chooses a book or a selection from a book and reads this aloud to the students.

Why is it important?

Reading to children is the single most important thing teachers and parents can do (Anderson, et al., 1984; Cunningham & Allington, 2002). Reading aloud to children is important for creating the motivation to become lifelong readers and learners (Cunningham, Hall, and Gambrell, 2002).

The following list contains key elements of this important classroom activity. It is not an all-inclusive list but rather a guide for observation.

	1	2	3
The teacher gathers the students close to him or her.			
The teacher introduces the book or material to be read (title, author, illustrator, cover picture or photography, etc.).			
The teacher reads aloud with enthusiasm and expression.			
The teacher talks about the pictures as he or she reads.			
The teacher talks and "thinks aloud" as he or she reads the text.			
The teacher talks about the book and makes links to his or her life, the students' lives, or books or topics discussed in class as he or she reads.			
The teacher ensures that all students are engaged in listening.			
After reading, the teacher talks about how the students could read this book, if it is chosen for independent reading (The teacher reviews the three ways to read: read the words, read the pictures, or retell the story).			
The teacher makes the book available (in a center, book basket, book tub, on a shelf, etc.)			
The lesson lasts as long as the children.			

1. Not observed in lesson.
2. Evidence from observation suggests that teacher may need additional support and practice.
3. Evidence from observation suggests that teacher is implementing with understanding.

Comments _____

_____

_____

Reading with Children

What is reading with children?

Teachers read with children when they use shared, choral, or echo reading. The shared reading of predictable big books is the process in which the teacher and children "share" the reading of a big book predictable by pictures or print. The echo and choral reading of nursery rhymes, traditional songs and poems, or predictable books is also part of reading with children.

Why is it important?

Big books simulate the "lap experience" where children can see both the pictures and the print. Reading and rereading a big book (a rhyme, song, or poem) offers children with little or no book experience the opportunity to be able to "pretend read" and develop the confidence that goes along with this accomplishment. Children with more book experiences begin to match words and print and some children can "really read" some selections (Hall and Cunningham, 1997; Hall and Williams, 2000).

The following two-page list contains key elements of this important classroom activity. It is not an all-inclusive list but rather a guide for observation.

	1	2	3
Before Reading:			
The teacher chooses a nursery rhyme, traditional song or poem, or a big book predictable by pictures and/or print.			
The teacher gathers the class close to him or her in the Big-Group area or "on the carpet" in the classroom.			
The teacher shows the chart page or book cover and talks about the title, author, cover, illustrator, and illustrations.			
The teacher builds prior knowledge needed to connect students to text prior to reading.			
The teacher takes a "picture walk" through the big book, talking about the pictures and any new words the class may encounter in this book.			
During Reading:			
The teacher reads the story (poem, song) aloud the first time.			
The children read the text (second and subsequent readings) using shared, echo, or choral reading.			

1. Not observed in lesson.
2. Evidence from observation suggests that teacher may need additional support and practice.
3. Evidence from observation suggests that teacher is implementing with understanding.

Comments _____

_____

The Administrator's Guide to Building Blocks™

After Reading:

	1	2	3
The teacher discusses the story with the students.			
If appropriate, the teacher works briefly and simply on a comprehension skill with the students.			

Examples:

	1	2	3
• Story Map—Talk about the characters, setting, and what happened at the beginning, middle, and end of the story.			
• "Doing the book" (acting it out)			
• Drawing the story			
If appropriate, the teacher can work on sentences, words, or letter sounds.			

Examples:

	1	2	3
• Sentence builders			
• Finding rhyming words			
• Finding familiar (high frequency) words			
• Finding words that begin like (beginning sounds)			
There is a before, during, and after reading phase of this lesson.			
The lesson lasts as long as the children.			
Classroom management is conducive to teaching this lesson.			

1. Not observed in lesson.
2. Evidence from observation suggests that teacher may need additional support and practice.
3. Evidence from observation suggests that teacher is implementing with understanding.

Comments _____

_____

_____

_____

_____

_____

_____

_____

_____

_____

_____

Children Reading by Themselves

What is children reading by themselves?
Children reading by themselves is when children are allowed to choose a book and read this book independently. In kindergarten, this also includes reading the pictures or retelling a story they have previously heard.

Why is it important?
Children learn to read by reading! Young children need opportunities to choose books they can read or pretend read. In kindergarten, this includes retelling a story in a book previously read to them or just looking at the pictures and telling the story (Anderson, et al., 1984; Hall and Williams, 2000; Cunningham, Hall, and Gambrell, 2002).

The following list contains key elements of this important classroom activity. It is not an all-inclusive list but rather a guide for observation. This activity takes place daily, but early in the year this activity may take place in the "reading" or "book" center and not all children may be in the center each day.

	1	2	3
The children have a comfortable place to sit and read.			
The teacher makes a variety of books available for children to choose from.			
The children are reading in a variety of ways: "real" reading, picture reading, and retelling stories that have been read to them before.			
The teacher provides stuffed animals or dolls for the children to "read" to.			
The teacher visits the Reading Center or reading area at some point and interacts with the children who are "reading" there.			
The teacher "oohs" and "aahs" over the books children are reading and the ways they are reading them.			
The children have opportunities to "read the room" (color words, number words, "Getting-to-Know-You" names, environmental print, predictable charts, interactive charts, etc.).			

1. Not observed in lesson.
2. Evidence from observation suggests that teacher may need additional support and practice.
3. Evidence from observation suggests that teacher is implementing with understanding.

Comments _____

_____

_____

Writing for Children

What is writing for children?
Teachers do the best teaching of writing in kindergarten when modeling what real writing looks like. Teachers write for children when they compose messages, charts, signs, and other types of authentic writing in front of their students.

Why is it important?
Writing for children is especially important to those students who come from homes where they have not seen someone writing for real reasons (Cunningham and Allington, 1998, 2002; Hall and Williams, 2000). However, all students will benefit from being shown what writing looks like and seeing the teacher thinking aloud as he or she writes (Morning Message or a journal entry at the end of the day).

The following two-page list contains key elements of this important classroom activity. It is not an all-inclusive list but rather a guide for observation.

	1	2	3
The teacher makes content decisions without input from the class.			
The teacher talks implicitly about the writing he or she is doing.			
During the modeling of writing, the teacher:			
• spells words aloud while writing.			
• explains use of punctuation.			
• describes formation of letters.			
• rereads as he or she writes.			
• uses one-to-one pointing as he or she reads.			
• uses terms such as: opening, closing, greeting, order.			
The teacher counts the sentences.			
The teacher counts the words in each sentence.			

1. Not observed in lesson.
2. Evidence from observation suggests that teacher may need additional support and practice.
3. Evidence from observation suggests that teacher is implementing with understanding.

Comments _____

_____

_____

_____

	1	2	3
The teacher compares the number of words in the sentences (more, less, same).			
The teacher counts the letters in each sentence.			
The teacher compares the numbers of letters in the sentences (more, less, same).			
Once writing and counting are completed, the teacher asks, "What do you notice?"			
• The teacher accepts the children's responses.			
• The teacher helps children find words that begin alike.			
• The teacher helps children find words that rhyme.			
The teacher asks children to find words they know (familiar or interesting-to-them words).			
The lesson lasts as long as the children.			

1. Not observed in lesson.
2. Evidence from observation suggests that teacher may need additional support and practice.
3. Evidence from observation suggests that teacher is implementing with understanding.

Comments _____

_____

_____

_____

_____

_____

_____

_____

_____

_____

_____

_____

_____

_____

_____

_____

_____

_____

_____

The Administrator's Guide to Building Blocks™

© Carson-Dellosa CD-2416

Writing with Children Using Predictable Charts

What is writing with children using predictable charts?

Predictable charts are weekly sources of writing opportunities for the kindergarten classroom. Because they play such an important role in the development of readers and writers in a Building-Blocks classroom, there is a separate checklist for this writing activity. Teachers build word recognition and concepts of print by following this weekly format.

Why is it important?

By using predictable charts, once called "structured language experience," all students will be able to participate, regardless of their own language skills. Students see themselves as readers and writers (Cunningham, 1979; Hall and Williams, 2000; Hall and Williams, 2001).

The following two-page list contains key elements of this important classroom activity. It is not an all-inclusive list but rather a guide for observation.

	1	2	3
Day One and Two—Sentence Dictation			
The sentence on the chart has a curricular tie (related to a book, field trip, holiday, etc.).			
The teacher models completing the predictable sentence by doing a sentence first.			
The children must state a complete sentence when giving their ending ("I would fly to Florida," not just "Florida.").			
The teacher models writing the sentences as the children dictate them.			
The child's name is placed in parentheses after his or her sentence.			
Each student contributes to the chart (may take two days).			
The lesson lasts as long as the children.			
Day Three—Touch Reading (Learning to Track Print)			
The teacher models the touch reading of the first (his or her) sentence.			
Each child "touch reads" his or her sentence on the chart.			
The teacher provides students with cut-up sentences on sentences strips.*			
Using a pocket chart, the teacher models matching words to text on the predictable chart with one of the cut-up sentences.*			
Using the pocket chart, two or three students match their cut-up sentences to the text on the predictable chart.*			
Each student will arrange his or her cut sentence to match the chart (on the floor or at his or her table/desk).*			
Each student touch reads his or her sentence to a partner or the teacher.*			
The lesson lasts as long as the children.			

* Time permitting after making several predictable charts.

	1	2	3
Day Four—Sentence Builders			
The teacher has prepared approximately three sentences from the chart before the lesson for the "sentence builders" activity.			
The teacher distributes the word cards for one sentence.			
Students with word cards come to the front of the class and "build" the sentence, matching the text on the predictable chart.			
The teacher and class read the sentence together while the teacher touches each child ("word") in the sentence.			
The teacher asks questions about the sentence ("Can you find a certain word? Can you find a word that begins like...? Rhymes with...?").			
The teacher repeats sentence builders with two (or more) sentences.			
The lesson lasts as long as the children.			
Day Five—Making a Class Book			
The teacher models arranging his or her own cut-up sentence and attaching it to a page for the class book. The teacher talks about what he or she will draw on the page above the sentence.			
The teacher distributes cut-up sentences to each child in the class.			
The children, sitting at their tables, arrange the words in their sentences in the correct order. Some may have to look at the predictable chart to be able to do this task.			
The teacher checks each child's sentence, and the child attaches his or her sentence to a page.			
Each child illustrates his or her own sentence page.			
The teacher assembles the pages into a class book (this may take place after the lesson is over).			
The lesson lasts as long as the children.			

1. Not observed in lesson.
2. Evidence from observation suggests that teacher may need additional support and practice.
3. Evidence from observation suggests that teacher is implementing with understanding.

Comments _____

_____

_____

_____

_____

_____

Children Writing by Themselves

What is children writing by themselves?

Children writing by themselves provides an opportunity for independent practice in writing. Students are allowed to write about topics of their choice. Daily time is allowed for students to write in a journal and/or work in a Writing Center.

Why is it important?

Students write best about the things they know (Calkins, 1986, 1994; Graves, 1983). Kindergarten students need opportunities to apply what they are learning about letters and sounds and aspects of writing learned when the teacher writes for and with students (Hall and Williams, 2000).

The following list contains key elements of this important classroom activity. It is not an all-inclusive list but rather a guide for observation.

	1	2	3
The Writing Center is open every day.			
The teacher provides a variety of materials in the Writing Center: pencils, markers, crayons, a variety of paper, note cards, computer, etc.			
The teacher accepts all writing attempts.			
The children are allowed to copy words found around the room.			
The children are encouraged to stretch out words and use "phonics spelling."			
The children are encouraged to "tell" about their stories.			
The teacher provides opportunities for children to share their writing on a regular basis.			
The children's writing is not edited by the teacher.			
During the first writing mini-lessons with the whole class, the teacher models the different ways kindergarten students can write (drawing, "driting," writing random letters, writing letters they hear in words, writing words they know, etc.			
If the teacher has the technology to allow her to model writing on the computer, he or she talks about where the space bar, punctuation keys, and shift key are located; how to make capital letters, etc.			
The lesson lasts as long as the children.			

1. Not observed in lesson.
2. Evidence from observation suggests that teacher may need additional support and practice.
3. Evidence from observation suggests that teacher is implementing with understanding.

Comments _____

_____

_____

Phonemic Awareness

What is phonemic awareness?

Phonemes are the smallest parts of speech. Phonemic awareness refers to developing students' ability to hear these parts (sounds) of words, separate the sounds, put them back together, and then change them to make new words (Adams, 1990; Yopp, 1992; Cunningham, 2000). Phonemic awareness is developed orally without print.

Why is it important?

Phonemic awareness has been shown to be an indicator of reading success. The more students play with words orally, the more successful they will be reading them (Snow, Burns, and Griffin, 1998).

The following list contains key phonemic awareness activities. These activities should be seen in other reading and writing checklists, as phonemic awareness is best taught in the context of real reading and writing. One or more of the following, but not all, may be observed in a lesson. It is not an all-inclusive list but rather a guide for observation.

	1	2	3
The teacher reads and discusses with children literature that focuses on some play with the sounds of language, including rhyming books, alphabet books, finger plays, songs, and poetry.			
The children learn and recite nursery rhymes.			
The teacher uses tongue twisters to teach beginning sounds.			
The children play with the beginning sounds of words ("*Kangaroo* starts like *Kaitlin.* What else starts like *kangaroo* and *Kaitlin?*").			
The children play with rhyming words ("*Bat* and *cat* rhyme. Does *rat* rhyme with *bat* and *cat?*").			
The teacher uses the Morning Message to discuss words that begin with the same sounds or have the same rhyme in them.			
The children "clap" words into separate syllables (one clap for each syllable: Joey = 2 syllables = 2 claps).			

1. Not observed in lesson.
2. Evidence from observation suggests that teacher may need additional support and practice.
3. Evidence from observation suggests that teacher is implementing with understanding.

Comments _____

_____

_____

Letters and Sounds

What is letters and sounds?
Letters and sounds refers to identifying the names and sounds of the letters of the alphabet.

Why is it important?
Children that can identify the names and sounds of the letters of the alphabet have a foundation that will help them as they later learn sight words and how to decode new words (Adams, 1990; Yopp, 1992; Snow, Burns, and Griffin, 1998). A child's level of letter and sound learning is correlated to his or her reading success.

The following list contains key letters and sounds activities. These activities should be seen in other reading and writing checklists as letters and sounds are best taught in the context of real reading and writing. One or more of the following, but not all, may be observed in a lesson. It is not an all-inclusive list but rather a guide for observation.

	1	2	3
The teacher uses "Getting-to-Know-You" activities to provide the foundation for learning most letter names and sounds (The "j" sound is taught when *Jason* is the student of the day and is interviewed in the "Getting-to-Know-You" activities).			
The teacher is sure to teach letters and sounds during real reading and writing activities (predictable charts, Morning Message, shared reading, and student writing). He or she does not use worksheets and workbooks.			
The teacher reads and discusses literature with the children that focuses on some play with the sounds of language (including rhyming books, alphabet books, and poetry).			
The teacher reads big books with students so that they can focus on words that begin alike.			
The teacher reads aloud alphabet books and makes them available for children to read.			
The teacher discusses beginning sounds of familiar words (days of the week, student names, etc.).			
The teacher writes the Morning Message with students so that letter names and sounds can be identified.			
The teacher prints tongue twisters so letter names and sounds can be discussed.			

1. Not observed in lesson.
2. Evidence from observation suggests that teacher may need additional support and practice.
3. Evidence from observation suggests that teacher is implementing with understanding.

Comments _____

_____

Interesting Words

What is interesting words?

Interesting words refers to helping students learn some "interesting-to-them words" like names, restaurants, cereals, sports teams, etc., that will help them later as they learn other words that begin with the same letters and sounds.

Why is it important?

Children who can read some words store letter name and sound knowledge in the associative memory making it easier for them to retrieve the information and use it in another learning situation (Cunningham, 2000; Hall and Cunningham, 1997; Hall and Williams, 2000).

The following list contains key activities for learning words. These activities should be seen in other reading and writing checklists, as words are best taught in the context of real reading and writing. One or more of the following, but not all, may be observed in a lesson. It is not an all-inclusive list but rather a guide for observation.

	1	2	3
The teacher uses "Getting-to-Know-You" activities to introduce children to one another, to help teach letters and sounds, and to help students learn to identify the names of the other children in class.			
The teacher introduces capital and lowercase letters during "Getting to Know You" activities, Morning Message, and predictable charts.			
The teacher uses print, in the form of classroom labels, books, posters, and student work, throughout the room.			
The teacher uses environmental print (cereal boxes, restaurant bags and cups, road signs, and professional and collegiate sports team products) to introduce children to commonly seen words.			
The teacher displays developmentally appropriate Word Walls in the classroom. Early in the year, Word Walls contain students' names and/or common environmental print (cereals, logos, etc.).			

1. Not observed in lesson.
2. Evidence from observation suggests that teacher may need additional support and practice.
3. Evidence from observation suggests that teacher is implementing with understanding.

Comments _____

_____

_____

Early in the Year
A Glance at a Typical Week's Lessons
for
Reading

Monday

During Big Group, the teacher reads a book about fall and colors aloud to the children, since the class has been talking about these two topics. The book she chooses is *Frederick* by Leo Lionni.

Later in the day, the class does a shared reading of the book *Brown Bear, Brown Bear, What Do You See?* by Bill Martin, Jr. This is the first day, so the teacher talks about the cover and asks the children what they think this book will be about. The teacher reads the book to the children, so they can hear and enjoy the story. She then reads it a second time and encourages the children to join in and share the reading. After reading the teacher uses the children's names to dismiss them, "Joey, Joey, what do you see?" He answers, "I see a book looking at me." The teacher continues, "Michelle, Michelle, what do you see?"

The Reading Center is open and children are in the center reading their self-selected books.

Tuesday

The teacher reads aloud the book *I Went Walking* by Susan Williams and compares this book to *Brown Bear, Brown Bear, What Do You See?*

For shared reading, the teacher continues with the big book, *Brown Bear, Brown Bear, What Do You See?* Before reading she restores prior knowledge by allowing students to retell the story during a picture walk through the book. The teacher and the class do a choral reading of the book together. The teacher stops after each page and discusses the dialogue. The teacher highlights what is said on each page with highlighting tape. After reading, the students read the highlighted parts and discuss words they know.

The Reading Center is open and children are in the center reading their self-selected books.

Wednesday

The teacher reads aloud the book *Color Zoo* by Lois Ehlert. The teacher has the class talk about the colors, shapes, and animals in the book.

For shared reading, the teacher continues with the big book, *Brown Bear, Brown Bear, What Do You See?* Before reading, she has a child retell the story. The teacher has covered a word on each page and together they read each page to find the covered word. For each page, the teacher asks, "Who thinks they can find the missing word in the pocket chart?" She makes sure to have the student explain the strategy used to determine her choice. The teacher then reveals the covered word and rereads the page. The lesson ends with the teacher and the class discussing the story. ("Who is this story about? Who does he ask to be his friend? Can you name them all?").

The Reading Center is open and children are in the center reading their self-selected books.

Thursday

The teacher reads aloud the book *Zoo-Looking* by Mem Fox and the class discusses the animals in this book compared to the animals in *Brown Bear, Brown Bear, What Do You See?*

For Shared Reading the teacher continues with the big book, *Brown Bear, Brown Bear, What Do You See?* The teacher has names of animals and the color words written on cards. Before reading, the children are asked to match the animals and the color words. The teacher asks, "What animal is on this page?" She has a student locate the card with the animal name on it. She asks, "What color is the animal on this page?" She has another student locate the card with the color on it. She then pairs the animal name and color word together in the pocket chart. The students do another choral reading. This time the class is divided in half. One half of the class reads the question while the other half of the class reads the answer. After reading, the teacher mixes up the word cards and has students, one by one, match an animal and color without her help. She lets them use the big book to check their pairings if they want or need to do that.

The Reading Center is open and children are in the center reading their self-selected books.

Friday

The teacher reads aloud another book by Bill Martin Jr., *Polar Bear, Polar Bear, What Do You Hear?* which uses a pattern similar to *Brown Bear, Brown Bear, What Do You See?* She discusses this pattern with the students.

For shared reading, the teacher continues with the big book, *Brown Bear, Brown Bear, What Do You See?* Before reading, the teacher tells the class they will have a "play" or "do the book" today. They begin the lesson with a picture walk discussing each page, what is happening, and who will play the part of that page's animal. The teacher and class do another choral reading. This time the child chosen to be the mouse and the other animals stand and mimic their parts on each page. The teacher repeats this until all children have had a chance to have a part in this "play."

The Reading Center is open and children are in the center reading their self-selected books.

Early in the Year
A Glance at a Typical Week's Lessons
for
Writing

Monday

The teacher writes *for* children early in the morning when she writes the Morning Message right after Big Group:

> Dear Class,
> Today is Monday.
> We will have a special visitor today.
> Love,
> Mrs. Arens

The teacher writes *for* children a second time just before they leave. This time she writes a journal entry at the end of the day:

> October 22, 2002
> We had P. E. today.
> In Science we are learning about fall.

The teacher writes *with* the children when they write a predictable chart. On the first day, she begins by writing her sentence and approximately half the children dictate sentences for her. She writes:

> In Fall
> I see scarecrows. (Mrs. Arens)
> I see pumpkins. (Merrill Kaye)
> I see colored leaves. (Alex)
> I see acorns. (John)

The Writing Center is open for children to write *by themselves*. Students may be copying October words, "driting," drawing pictures and pretend writing, etc. Janet, Lynn, and Kim will share a selection of their writing with the class.

Tuesday

The first time the teacher writes *for* children is right after Big Group when she writes the Morning Message:

> Dear Class,
> Today is Tuesday.
> We are getting ready for our field trip
> to the orchard.
> Love,
> Mrs. Arens

The teacher writes *for* children a second time just before the students leave. She writes a journal entry at the end of the day:

> October 23, 2002
> We gathered beautiful leaves from outside.
> They are red, yellow, and orange.

The teacher writes *with* the children and finishes the predictable chart they started yesterday:

> I see haystacks. (Lafe)
> I see football games. (Jeff)
> I see apples. (Tracy)
> I see acorns. (Amanda)
> I see

The Writing Center is open for children to write *by themselves*. Students may be copying October words, "driting," drawing pictures and pretend writing, etc. Lafe, Elinor, and Tracy will share a selection of their writing with the class.

The Administrator's Guide to Building Blocks™

Wednesday

The teacher writes *for* children three times today. The first time is right after Big Group when she writes the Morning Message:

> Dear Class,
> Today is Wednesday.
> We have a new center today.
> It is the Store Center.
> Love,
> Mrs. Arens

The teacher writes *for* children a second time when she writes a sign for a center and reads it to the children. The sign says: The Store Center.

> The Store Center
> 1. Make a list.
> 2. Help take money.
> 3. Put snacks in a cart.

The third time she writes *for* children is just before the children leave. She writes a journal entry at the end of the day:

> October 24, 2002
> Erin's mom came in to tell us how pumpkins are grown. The pumpkin bread she made for us was delicious.

The teacher wrote *with* the children when they worked on a predictable chart Monday and Tuesday. All the children "touch read" their sentences today. Then, they match cut-up sentences to the sentences on the chart.

The Writing Center is open for children to write *by themselves*. Students may be copying October words, "driting," drawing pictures and pretend writing, etc. Lynn, Rhonda, and Alex will share a selection of their writing with the class.

Thursday

The teacher writes *for* children twice today. The first time is right after big group when she writes the Morning Message for the children:

```
Dear Class,
Today is Thursday.
Katie has a surprise to remind us of fall.
What could it be?
Love,
Mrs. Arens
```

The second time she writes *for* children is just before the children leave. She writes a journal entry at the end of the day:

```
October 25, 2002
The orchard was so much fun.
Apples grow in the fall, too.
Devon and Elinor liked the green apples best.
```

The teacher wrote *with* the children when they worked on a predictable chart Monday and Tuesday. Today, the children do "Sentence Builders," building four sentences the teacher chose.

The Writing Center is open for children to write *by themselves*. Students may be copying October words, "driting," drawing pictures and pretend writing, etc. Sue, Dana, and Eric will share a selection of their writing with the class.

Friday

The teacher writes *for* children twice today. The first time is right after big group when she writes the Morning Message for the children:

> Dear Class,
> Today is Friday.
> It is William's birthday.
> He brought in some treats for snack.
> Love,
> Mrs. Arens

The second time she writes *for* children is just before the children leave. She writes a journal entry at the end of the day:

> October 26, 2002
> We made beautiful apple prints today.
> We used the colors of apples: red,
> yellow, and green. They were so pretty!

The teacher wrote *with* the children when they worked on a predictable chart Monday and Tuesday. Today, each child makes a page for a class book by pasting his sentence on a piece of paper and illustrating it.

The Writing Center is open for children to write *by themselves*. Students may be copying October words, "driting," drawing pictures and pretend writing, etc. They share their class book *In Fall* with another class today.

Early in the Year
A Glance at a Typical Week's Lessons
for
Phonemic Awareness, Letters and Sounds, and Interesting Words

Monday

The Morning Message is written with the children during the opening. It tells the class that the person of the day is MacKenzie and that they have music today. The teacher emphasizes that MacKenzie and music start with the same sound.

MacKenzie's name is introduced in the "Getting-to-Know-You" activities. The children say the letters in her name and chant them. The letters are counted and the M is highlighted as the beginning sound. The children "clap" the syllables in MacKenzie and find that there are three parts to her name. Next, MacKenzie completes the "Getting-to-Know-You" interactive chart. MacKenzie's name is added to the Name Wall under Matt.

Today's story is the big book *Miss Mary Mack* by Mary Ann Hoberman. Children chant the rhyme with the teacher during the second reading. The teacher guides children to notice that "Miss," "Mary," and "Mack" all start like MacKenzie.

Tuesday

Today during the Morning Message, the children learn that Whitney is the person of the day and that they have P. E.

Whitney's name is introduced in the "Getting-to-Know-You" activities. The children say, chant, and count the letters in her name. The children discover that Whitney has two parts when they clap and say her name. Next, Whitney completes the "Getting-to-Know-You" interactive chart. Whitney's name is the first "W" name on the Name Wall.

Today's story is *The Z Was Zapped: A Play in Twenty-Six Acts* by Chris Van Allsburg. Names from the Name Wall are matched to the letters of the alphabet in the book during the second reading.

After the story, children sing the song "Teacher" (to the tune of "Bingo"). The /c/ sound and the -at ending are sung, not the names of the letters.

There was a teacher who had a pet and cat was its name-o.

/c/   /c/   /c/   -at

/c/   /c/   /c/   -at

/c/   /c/   /c/   -at

And cat was its name-o.

Other verses are sung as children suggest animal names.

Wednesday

Today's person of the day is Trey, and the children go to art.

Trey's name is introduced in the "Getting-to-Know-You" activities. The children say, chant, and count the letters in his name. The children discover that Trey has one part when they clap and say his name. Next, Trey completes the "Getting-to-Know-You" interactive chart. Trey's name is the third "T" name on the Name Wall.

Today, the children learn a new nursery rhyme, "Higglety Pigglety, Pop!" from *Read Aloud Rhymes for the Very Young* by Jack Prelutsky. Children chime in with the rhymes on the second and third readings.

After reading "Higglety Pigglety, Pop!" children complete the predictable chart, "I hurry to..."

```
                    I Hurry
      I hurry to lunch. (Mrs. Loman)
      I hurry to recess. (Jurhee)
      I hurry to dinner. (Chris)
      I hurry to play. (Howard)
```

Thursday

Today's person of the day is Kyla, and the children go to music.

Kyla's name is introduced in the "Getting-to-Know-You" activities. The children say, chant, and count the letters in her name. The children discover that Kyla's name has two parts when they clap and say it. Next, Kyla completes the "Getting-to-Know-You" interactive chart. Her name is the third "K" name on the Name Wall.

The children learn a tongue twister: Karl Kessler kept the ketchup in the kitchen. They change the names in the tongue twister to the names of some children in their classroom.

```
      Kyla and Kaitlin kept the ketchup in the kitchen.
      Kyla and Keith kept the ketchup in the kitchen.
      Kaitlin and Keith kept the ketchup in the kitchen.
```

The ABC book read today is *The Alphabet Tree* by Leo Lionni. Children stand up as the teacher reads the pages that start with the same sound as their names.

Children read their sentences on the predictable chart. Kyla, Trey, and Whitney match their cut-up sentences to their sentences on the chart.

Friday

Today's person of the day is Chad, and children go to P. E.

Chad's name is introduced in the "Getting-to-Know-You" activities. The children say, chant, and count the letters in his name. The children discover that Chad has one part when they clap and say his name. Chad completes the "Getting-to-Know-You" interactive chart. His name is the first "C" name on the Name Wall.

The children look at the cereal boxes and logos they brought in for environmental print samples. They are looking for things that begin with /ch/. The teacher slowly reads the name of the product on each box. They find a box of Cheerios®. Students watch as the teacher cuts the name from the box and places it in the pocket chart. The children chant the letter names with the teacher, then write Cheerios® on the back of the paper that they wrote Chad and drew his picture.

The children read their sentences on the predictable chart. The teacher uses some of their sentences (Chad's, MacKenzie's, and Kaitlin's) as she invites children up to be "sentence builders."

Teacher's Planning Checklists

Early in the Year

A few words of caution about the use of the following pages...

The checklists offered in this book are intended to convey the basics of the Building-Blocks™ Literacy Model for kindergarten. The model is not rigidly defined, especially as teachers gain confidence in the delivery and begin to interject more of their own personalities and creativity. However, some elements define the model, provide the careful balance, are multilevel, and ensure a greater level of success. These checklists are offered in response to administrators and teachers who have asked for more specific details in an attempt to do a better job of getting the Building-Blocks™ Model started.

Also, when the checklists mention that the lessons "last as long as the children," it is a reference to ending the lessons when the children are no longer engaged in learning.

Reading to Children

As I prepare and present lessons for reading to children early in the year, I am sure to . . .

_____ 1. Provide a good model of fluency in reading and attempt to motivate students through a daily teacher read-aloud. My read-aloud was clear, expressive, and enthusiastic.

_____ 2. Promote reading through teacher read-alouds and talk about books at one or several appropriate times throughout the day.

_____ 3. Model the types of questions during closure time that will lead young students to think about and discuss the story.

_____ 4. Connect the read-alouds, when possible, to a subject, theme, or concept that the class has studied, is studying, or will study in the near future.

_____ 5. Connect the read-alouds, when possible, to my life, the students' lives, and/or the real world.

_____ 6. Make the lesson last as long as the children.

Reading with Children

As I prepare and present lessons for reading with children early in the year, I am sure to . . .

_____ 1. Choose a familiar nursery rhyme, song, poem, or a big book predictable by pictures or print.

_____ 2. Provide activities or discussion before reading to prepare the children for what they will read (setting, characters, vocabulary, etc.).

_____ 3. Give the children a first reading which is clear, expressive, and enthusiastic.

_____ 4. Reread the story or selection several times using shared, echo, or choral reading with all children joining in.

_____ 5. Provide activities after reading to help the children understand what they read (talk about the story, sequence the events, act it out, draw, etc.).

_____ 6. Work with high-frequency words or rhyming words used in the story (sentence builders, finding high-frequency words, finding rhyming words, etc.).

_____ 7. Help students become aware of letters and sounds (letter/sounds of some important words, words that start alike, etc.).

_____ 8. Compare the book or story to another book or story read previously.

_____ 9. Make a souvenir (art activity) to help remember the story and as a retelling prompt.

_____ 10. Make the lesson last as long as the children.

Children Reading by Themselves

As I prepare and present lessons for children reading by themselves early in the year, I am sure to . . .

_____ 1. Provide an adequate supply of books and other reading materials on various topics, of different genres, and on varied reading levels appropriate for kindergarten students. I place the materials in the Reading Center.

_____ 2. Introduce the Reading Center to the class and let some children visit it daily.

_____ 3. Spend time in the Reading Center listening to and encouraging children's reading.

_____ 4. Let children choose how they want to read their books to me (read the words, read the pictures, or retell the story).

_____ 5. "Ooh" and "aah" at children's real reading or pretend reading.

_____ 6. Start letting my class spend a few (three to five) minutes with books.

_____ 7. Increase my time gradually each week; my goal is 15 minutes.

_____ 8. Make the lesson last as long as the children.

Writing for Children

As I prepare and present lessons in writing for children early in the year, I am sure to . . .

_____ 1.   Make decisions on what I write about.

_____ 2.   Talk or think aloud while I am writing.

_____ 3.   Write, and while I am writing, I:

___ spell words aloud.

___ explain use of punctuation.

___ describe the formation of letters.

___ reread the message as I write.

___ use one-to-one pointing as I read.

___ use terms such as _greeting, closing, word, letter, sentence, period, question mark, exclamation point,_ etc.

_____ 4.   Assist the class in counting the words in the sentences.

_____ 5.   Assist the class in comparing the words in the sentences.

_____ 6.   Assist the class in counting the number of letters in a sentence.

_____ 7.   Ask the class to compare the numbers of letters in the sentences.

_____ 8.   Ask the students to tell me what they notice about the writing.

_____ 9.   Accept the responses the children give.

_____ 10. Ask the children to find words they know.

_____ 11. Make the lesson last as long as the children.

The Administrator's Guide to Building Blocks™

Writing with Children Using Predictable Charts

As I prepare and present five-day lessons early in the year for writing with children using predictable charts, I am sure to . . .

Day One and Two

_____ 1.   Decide on a curricular tie-in for our class predictable chart.

_____ 2.   Begin by modeling my own sentence.

_____ 3.   Ask each student to say the complete sentence. ("I would fly to Chicago.")

_____ 4.   Write each sentence in front of the class.

_____ 5.   Make the lesson last as long as the children.

Day Three

_____ 1.   Prepare cut-up sentences for each student.

_____ 2.   Touch read my sentence first.

_____ 3.   Ask each child to touch read his or her sentence.

_____ 4.   Choose one of the cut-up sentences to model matching text on the chart.

_____ 5.   Ask two or three students to match their sentences with the text on the chart, as the class watches.

_____ 6.   Observe as each child (at his or her seat or on the floor) matches his or her sentence with the text on the chart.

_____ 7.   Observe as each child touch reads his or her sentence to a partner or me.

_____ 8.   Make the lesson last as long as the children.

Day Four

_____ 1. Prepare word cards for at least three sentences.

_____ 2. Randomly distribute word cards, giving one card per child.

_____ 3. Ask students to come forward and build the sentence by matching the text on the pocket chart.

_____ 4. Lead the children in reading the sentence as I touch the head of each child (word) in the sentence.

_____ 5. Ask questions, such as:

___ "Can you find the word *like*?"

___ "Can you find a word that begins like *Merrill*?"

___ "Can you find a word that rhymes with *will*?"

_____ 6. Make the lesson last as long as the children.

Day Five

_____ 1. Arrange my cut-up sentences on a large page (piece of chart paper) and either draw or describe what I will draw to match my words. I demonstrate gluing the words in order on the page.

_____ 2. Provide each student with a cut-up sentence.

_____ 3. Observe while students arrange the sentences on their pages.

_____ 4. Check for accuracy before each student glues the words to the page.

_____ 5. Observe as children illustrate their pages.

_____ 6. Assemble the pages into a class book.

_____ 7. Make the lesson last as long as the children.

Children Writing by Themselves

As I prepare and present lessons early in the year for children writing by themselves , I am sure to . . .

_____ 1. Model for my kindergarten students the different ways they could write in kindergarten (drawing, "driting," writing random letters, writing words, writing sentences).

_____ 2. Think aloud as I write my mini-lesson.

_____ 3. Verbalize what I am doing and why as I write my mini-lesson.

_____ 4. Find words around the room that I can copy. I also stretch out words and write the sounds I hear, writing one or two words in their "phonics" or sound spelling as a model for the children.

_____ 5. Model how to choose a topic or allow students to write about what I write about.

_____ 6. Coach my students when they are ready to write.

_____ 7. Not spell for my students but let them do the work.

_____ 8. Allow my students to compose on the computer (if one is available).

_____ 9. Provide opportunities for my students to share their writing.

_____ 10. Make the lesson last as long as the children.

Phonemic Awareness

As I prepare and present lessons for phonemic awareness early in the year, I am sure to . . .

_____ 1. Use literature that focuses on some play with the sounds of language, including rhyming books, alphabet books, finger plays, songs, and poetry.

_____ 2. Read and discuss books, songs, or poems with children.

_____ 3. Have children read, learn, and recite nursery rhymes.

_____ 4. Have children play with the beginning sounds of words ("*Kangaroo* starts like *Kaitlin*. What else starts like *kangaroo* and *Kaitlin*?").

_____ 5. Use tongue twisters to teach beginning sounds.

_____ 6. Have children play with rhyming words ("*Bat* and *cat* rhyme. Does *rat* rhyme with *bat* and *cat*?").

_____ 7. Use the Morning Message to discuss words that begin with the same sounds or rhyme.

_____ 8. Have children "clap" words into separate syllables (one clap for each syllable: Joey = 2 syllables = 2 claps).

Letters and Sounds

As I prepare and present lessons for letters and sounds early in the year, I am sure to . . .

_____ 1. Use "Getting-to-Know-You" activities to provide the foundation for learning most letter names and sounds (The "j" sound is taught when *Jason* is the student of the day and is interviewed in the "Getting-to-Know-You" activities.).

_____ 2. Teach letters and sounds during real reading and writing activities (predictable charts, Morning Message, shared reading, and student writing). I do not use worksheets and workbooks.

_____ 3. Read and discuss literature that focuses on some play with the sounds of language, including rhyming books, alphabet books, and poetry.

_____ 4. Read big books with students and focus on words that begin alike.

_____ 5. Read alphabet books to children and make them available for children to read.

_____ 6. Discuss the beginning sounds of familiar words (days of the week, student names, etc.).

_____ 7. Write the Morning Message with students and identify letter names and sounds.

_____ 8. Print tongue twisters and discuss letter names along with letter sounds.

Interesting Words

As I prepare and present lessons for interesting words early in the year, I am sure to . . .

_____ 1. Use "Getting-to-Know-You" activities to introduce children to one another, to help teach letters and sounds, and to help students learn to identify the names of the other children in class.

_____ 2. Introduce capital and lowercase letters during "Getting-to-Know-You" activities, Morning Message, and predictable charts.

_____ 3. Display print, in the form of classroom labels, books, posters, and student work, throughout the room.

_____ 4. Display environmental print (cereal boxes, restaurant logos, road signs, professional and collegiate sports team products, etc.) to introduce children to commonly seen words.

_____ 5. Display developmentally appropriate Word Walls. Early in the year, Word Walls contain students' names (Name Wall) and/or common environmental print from cereal boxes, logos, etc. (Environmental Print Wall).

Errors, Misunderstandings, and Weaknesses Most Commonly Observed in Implementing Buildings Blocks

Reading

1. **Not reading aloud to kindergarten students every day**
   Some teachers want to read aloud every day, but on some days the time gets away from them and before they know it, the students are going home. Teachers need to set aside a special time each day (during Big Group, right after recess or outside playtime, when returning from lunch, etc.) for this activity. By setting aside a special time to read aloud each day, teachers never miss a day.

2. **Not becoming familiar with a book before it is read**
   Teachers are familiar with most of the books they read aloud. However, reading a new book often requires a short period of time for the teacher to get "comfortable" with the book before reading it to the students. Spending a few minutes with a new book allows teachers to have both an interesting and effective teacher read-aloud.

3. **Not having a special place to read aloud to students**
   Having a special chair for the teacher to sit in and a rug for the children to sit on will make the read aloud time inviting and special. It also gives the children the message that this is an important activity for everyone involved.

4. **Forgetting to introduce the book with a few comments**
   Teachers make the book special when they introduce it with a few comments. Tell something about the book, the author, or why you chose the book to read aloud. With informational text the teacher needs to show the table of contents, headings, charts, pictures, etc. This will give students a little preview of what is to come when he or she introduces the book.

5. **Choosing a book to read aloud that is too long for the student's attention span, or not breaking a long book or story into two or more sessions**
Early in the year, some kindergarten students have short attention spans and their listening skills are not well developed yet. There are many books that are just right for these young listeners and when a book or story appears to be too long, then these stories can be broken into two or more sessions—even young children need to learn to listen to a story over several days.

6. **Choosing a book for shared reading that is not predictable by pictures or print**
Some good stories have too much print on the page to talk about the text while reading. Materials like these can be read to the children but should not be chosen for shared reading.

7. **Not having before, during, and after reading activities**
To help kids focus on reading for meaning, a teacher should prepare before, during, and after reading activities. Whatever the teacher talks about before reading (characters, setting, prediction, sequence, etc.) is what the teacher would follow up on after reading it.

8. **Not reading and rereading a story several times**
Often children who could not read the text the first time they saw it will be able to read the text after several readings.

9. **Not starting off slowly with independent reading**
Children just need a few (three to five) minutes the first few weeks of "self-selected" or independent reading. This time increases as the year goes on.

10. **Not reminding the children each day that there are more ways to read than just reading the words**
Children need to know that it is all right to look at or "read" the pictures and "tell" the story, or "pretend read" a story they have heard before.

Errors, Misunderstandings, and Weaknesses Most Commonly Observed in Implementing Buildings Blocks

Writing

1. Stopping the Morning Message

Some teachers will stop writing a Morning Message once the students are used to the format and questions. They lose an important part of the lesson—letting students help write the message (interactive writing) when they are ready. The activity can be made more challenging by changing the form and types of sentences, and changing what questions the students are asked.

2. Not writing in front of the children

Children need to see how people write. Some teachers will write the Morning Message on the board when the children are not in the room watching. Some teachers write the predictable part (I saw a…) of a predictable chart before school to "save time." They lose an important part of the lesson—letting the students see that what they say, they can write.

3. Spelling words for students

Some students will continue to ask for words to be spelled. Once this pattern of spelling for them begins, the students will become dependent on assistance. They will not call up and write what they know about the sounds they hear and the letters that represent those sounds. Thus, the teacher is doing the work, not the students.

4. Editing kindergarten writing

Many kindergarten students will struggle to read their writing in edited form. They write words as they hear them and when changed to standard spelling, the child may no longer "know" what he or she has written. The process of editing may also make students feel they are not *real* writers decreasing their production. The teacher's job in the kindergarten is to be a cheerleader, not an editor!

5. Pushing students to write conventionally

Model, model, model! However, when it comes time for independent writing by students, let them write. Observing students' writing behaviors allows the teacher to assess their stages of writing/spelling development and what aspects need further instruction. Coaching a child is encouraging them and assisting them one-on-one. A large portion of writing instruction in kindergarten occurs during writing to and with children.

6. Using lined paper

For many kindergarten children, fine motor skills have not developed. Mandating that these young children use lined paper makes writing too hard a task. If some children are ready to write on lined paper, then that could be a "choice" for those children. Some teachers feel pressured to use lined paper to "prepare" their children for first grade. If this is the case, delay that exposure until the final few weeks of kindergarten. If teachers have modeled letter formation daily during the year, the children's handwriting will be appropriate, and the transition to handwriting paper will not be a difficult one.

7. **Not allowing students to write until formal handwriting instruction on all the letters of the alphabet has been completed**

   Teachers provide constant modeling of letter formation during the writing for students (Morning Message, journal entry, predictable charts, etc.) The "Getting-to-Know-You" lessons at the beginning of the year provide ample opportunity to begin the letter formation instruction. Valuable time will be lost if teachers wait for a "formal" introduction to each letter.

8. **Mandating topics**

   Students are able to write better and in greater amounts when they write about the things that matter most to them. If we require a certain topic to be addressed, that topic may appeal to one student, while leaving another to wonder what to say. Use mini-lessons to suggest topics and give tips on how to decide about a topic. Offering suggestions and mandating topics to be covered are very different forms of instruction.

9. **Not allowing students to write on the same topic as the idea presented in the mini-lesson**

   Many students will gravitate to the same topic as the one the teacher has written about during the mini-lesson. The mini-lesson is done to provide ideas for writing. If a student consistently writes on the same topic as the teacher, then it would be a great time to do a mini-lesson on how to choose topics. Students need to be encouraged to find the things that matter most to them to focus on in writing. However, we will also have students who have such limited experiences they will search for models and ideas.

10. **Not allowing copying from the room**

    In any one room, the range of developmental levels of writing will be broad throughout the year. (Hall and Cunningham, 1997). For some students, the stage they will feel the most comfort in will result in copying from the Morning Message, predictable charts, and the print that covers the walls in the classroom. It is a stage many kindergarten children will move through in the process of learning to write. Especially early in the year, copying may be what a student can and will do.

11. **Writing the standard spelling underneath a child's words**

    If a teacher writes words underneath the child's writing to remember what was written, the child perceives that their writing is not real writing. The teacher may even say, "This is how it is written in books." The message is still the same. A good strategy to try is writing *in cursive* on a small self-stick note and attaching it to the back of the page. This will help the teacher to remember the text at a later date without discouraging young authors.

12. **Not taking time to celebrate all writing attempts**

    Watching a young child write is a fascinating experience. The development of fine motor skills, the knowledge of letter/sound relationships, the knowledge of our language, and the conventions of writing are all developing simultaneously. That alone is a reason to celebrate! It is critical that young writers view themselves as successful in writing. Celebrate within your classroom community, your school community, and the community where you live. Writing has an inherent value worth celebrating!

Errors, Misunderstandings, and Weaknesses Most Commonly Observed in Implementing Buildings Blocks

Phonemic Awareness, Letters and Sounds, and Interesting Words

1. **Expecting children to know all the letter names and sounds too early in the year and not providing enough time for children to develop phonemic awareness**

   Children need to be able to hear the sounds in words before attaching a name and symbol (letter) to it. It is impossible for children to label a sound they can't *hear* (segment the sound from the rest of the word). It is also important to recognize that once print has been added to a phonemic awareness activity it becomes a phonics activity. It is necessary to spend some time developing students' abilities to *hear* the sounds in words before children can label the letter name and sounds in words.

2. **Teaching letter names and sounds using a letter-of-the-week program**

   Students easily learn most letters and sounds by learning their classmates' names in the "Getting-to-Know-You" activities. These activities should be the basis for all work with letters and sounds. Letter-of-the-week programs tend to introduce children to obscure letter/sound connections ("r" stands for running rabbit) that may or may not be relevant or interesting to children. Nothing is more relevant or interesting than a child's friends. Students hear their friends' names called every day and see them written on papers, school boxes, books, backpacks, lunch boxes, etc. Those words, letters, and sounds are reinforced daily.

   The best way for children to learn about letters and sounds is to engage them in real reading and writing activities. Classroom activities such as predictable charts, Morning Message, shared reading, and student writing also reinforce letter/sound learning. The least efficient way to learn about letters and sounds is with workbooks and worksheets. Many of them use pictures that aren't meaningful to the children in the classroom and take up valuable learning time with activities such as coloring, cutting, and pasting that have nothing to do with learning letters and sounds.

3. Using traditional Word Walls and Word Wall activities in kindergarten

Kindergarten classrooms should be print-rich environments, not just rooms with words on one wall. All print should have meaning to the students and must be part of something they have been taught. A teacher may choose to display students' names on one wall. They may also choose to display the environmental print that children are learning. You should also see lists of color words and number words, as well as words and pictures connected to the month, theme, or topic being studied in the class.

There is never a time in kindergarten when children should have to recognize and spell words correctly using the Word Wall like they do in first grade. When kindergarten children are able to read and write, they should be encouraged to do so. They should be viewed as readers and writers and given appropriate opportunities to read and write. They should not be pushed to be first graders; they will be first graders next year!

Later in the year (fourth quarter), some teachers may choose to display some high-frequency words in or near the Writing Center. When a high-frequency word is added to this display, it should be only after students have had multiple exposures and experiences with the word (I, can, like, etc.). It is different from the Word Wall and Word Wall activities seen in grade one to five classrooms.

Administrator's Observation Checklists Later in the Year

A few words of caution about the use of the following pages…

The checklists offered in this book are intended to convey the basics of the Building-Blocks™ Literacy Model for kindergarten. The model is not rigidly defined, especially as teachers gain confidence in the delivery and begin to interject more of their own personalities and creativity. However, some elements define the model, provide the careful balance, are multilevel, and ensure a greater level of success. These checklists are offered in response to administrators and teachers who have asked for more specific details in an attempt to do a better job of getting the Building-Blocks™ Model started.

Also, when the checklists mention that "the lesson lasts as long as the children," it is a reference to ending the lesson when the children are no longer engaged in learning.

Reading to Children

What is reading to children?

Reading to children is when a teacher chooses a book or a selection from a book and reads this aloud to his or her students.

Why is it important?

Reading aloud to children is the single most important thing teachers and parents can do (Anderson et al, 1984). Reading to children is important for creating the motivation to become lifelong readers and learners (Cunningham, Hall, and Gambrell, 2002).

The following list contains key elements of this important classroom activity. It is not an all-inclusive list but rather a guide for observation.

	1	2	3
The teacher gathers the students close to him or her.			
The teacher introduces the book or material to be read (title, author, illustrator, cover picture/photography, etc.).			
The teacher reads aloud with enthusiasm and expression.			
The teacher talks about the pictures as he or she reads.			
The teacher talks and "thinks aloud" as he or she reads.			
The teacher talks about the book and makes links to his or her life, the students' lives, or books or topics discussed in class as he or she reads.			
The teacher ensures that all students are engaged in listening.			
The teacher reviews the three ways kindergarten children read: read the words, read the pictures, or retell the story.			
The teacher makes the book available (in a center, book basket, book tub, on a shelf, etc.) for the children to read.			
The lesson lasts as long as the children.			

1. Not observed in lesson.
2. Evidence from observation suggests that teacher may need additional support and practice.
3. Evidence from observation suggests that teacher is implementing with understanding.

Comments _____

_____

_____

_____

Reading with Children

What is reading with children?
Teachers read with children when they use shared, choral, or echo reading. The shared reading of predictable big books is a term used to describe the process in which the teacher and children "share" the reading of a predictable big book.

Why is it important?
Reading big books helps simulate the "lap experience" in which children can see both the pictures and the print. Reading and rereading a big book (a rhyme, song, or poem) offers children with little book experience the opportunity to be able to "pretend read" and develop the confidence that goes along with this accomplishment. Children with more book experiences begin to match words and print and some children can "really read" some selections (Hall and Cunningham, 1997; Hall and Williams, 2000).

The following two-page list contains key elements of this important classroom activity. It is not an all-inclusive list but rather a guide for observation.

	1	2	3
Before Reading:			
The teacher chooses a nursery rhyme, traditional song or poem, or a predictable big book.			
The teacher gathers the class close to him or her in the Big-Group area or "on the carpet" in the classroom.			
The teacher shows the chart page or book cover and talks about the title, author, cover, illustrator, and illustrations.			
The teacher builds prior knowledge needed to connect students to text prior to reading.			
The teacher takes a "picture walk" through the big book, talking about the pictures and any new words students may encounter in this book.			
During Reading:			
The teacher reads aloud the story (poem, song) the first time.			
The children read the text (second and subsequent readings) using shared, echo, or choral reading.			

1. Not observed in lesson
2. Evidence from observation suggests that teacher may need additional support and practice.
3. Evidence from observation suggests that teacher is implementing with understanding.

Comments _____

_____

_____

	1	2	3

After Reading:

The teacher discusses the story with students.			
If appropriate, the teacher works briefly and simply on a comprehension skill with the students.			

Examples:

• Story Map—Talk about the characters, setting, and what happened at the beginning, middle, and end of the story.			
• "Doing the book" (acting it out)			
• Drawing the story			
If appropriate, the teacher works on sentences, words, or letter sounds.			

Examples:

• Sentence builders			
• Finding rhyming words			
• Finding familiar (high frequency) words			
• Finding words that begin like (beginning sounds)			
The lesson lasts as long as the children.			
Classroom management is conducive to teaching this lesson.			

1. Not observed in lesson.
2. Evidence from observation suggests that teacher may need additional support and practice.
3. Evidence from observation suggests that teacher is implementing with understanding.

Comments _____

_____

_____

_____

_____

_____

_____

_____

_____

_____

_____

Children Reading by Themselves

What is children reading by themselves?
Children reading by themselves is when children are allowed to choose books and read these books by themselves. In kindergarten, this also includes reading the pictures or retelling a story the children have previously heard.

Why is it important?
Children learn to read by reading! Young children need opportunities to choose books they can read or pretend read. In kindergarten this includes retelling a story in a book previously read to them or just looking at the pictures and telling the story (Anderson et al, 1984; Cunningham Hall, and Gambrell, 2002).

The following two-page list contains key elements of this important classroom activity. It is not an all-inclusive list but rather a guide for observation. This activity takes place daily. Early in the year this activity may take place in the "reading" or "book" center and not all children may be in the center each day. Later in the year, the children are all engaged daily in self-selected reading.

	1	2	3
The teacher sets aside short periods of time daily (3-5 minutes initially; up to 15 minutes as the year progresses) for children to "read."			
The children have a comfortable place to sit and read.			
The teacher makes a variety of books available for children to choose from.			
The children are reading in a variety of ways: "real" reading, picture reading, and retelling stories that have been read to them before.			
The teacher provides stuffed animals or dolls for the children to "read" to.			

1. Not observed in lesson.
2. Evidence from observation suggests that teacher may need additional support and practice.
3. Evidence from observation suggests that teacher is implementing with understanding.

Comments _____

_____

_____

_____

_____

_____

The Administrator's Guide to Building Blocks™

	1	2	3
The teacher visits and interacts with several children who are "reading."			
The children are encouraged to read aloud to the teacher. The teacher "oohs" and "ahhs" over the books children are reading and the ways they are reading them.			
The children have opportunities to "read-the-room" (color words, number words, "Getting-to-know-You" names, environmental print, predictable charts, interactive charts, etc.) at some time during the day.			
The lessons lasts as long as the children.			

1. Not observed in lesson.
2. Evidence from observation suggests that teacher may need additional support and practice.
3. Evidence from observation suggests that teacher is implementing with understanding.

Comments _____

_____
_____
_____
_____
_____
_____
_____
_____
_____
_____
_____
_____
_____
_____
_____
_____
_____
_____
_____
_____
_____

Writing for Children

What is writing for children?

Teachers do the best teaching of writing in kindergarten when modeling what real writing looks like. Teachers write for children when they compose messages, charts, signs, and other types of authentic writing in front of their students.

Why is it important?

Writing for children is especially important to those students who come from homes where they have not seen someone writing for real reasons (Cunningham and Allington, 1998, 2002). However, all students will benefit from being shown what writing looks like and hearing the teacher think aloud as he or she writes (Morning Message, journal entry at the end of the day, and writing mini-lessons).

The following two-page list contains key elements of this important classroom activity. It is not an all-inclusive list but rather a guide for observation.

	1	2	3
The teacher makes content decisions with or without input from the class.			
The teacher talks implicitly about the writing he or she is doing.			
During the modeling of writing the teacher:			
• spells words aloud while writing.			
• claps word parts.			
• stretches out words.			
• explains use of punctuation.			
• asks students to assist in listening for sounds.			
• explains the use of capital letters.			
• describes the formation of letters.			
• defines return sweep when necessary.			
• rereads as he or she writes.			
• uses one-to-one pointing as he or she reads.			
• uses terms such as: opening, closing, greeting, order.			

1. Not observed in lesson.
2. Evidence from observation suggests that teacher may need additional support and practice.
3. Evidence from observation suggests that teacher is implementing with understanding.

Comments _____

_____

	1	2	3
Once writing is completed, teaching points could be:			
• counting the sentences.			
• counting the words or letters in each sentence.			
• comparing the number of letters to words in the sentences (more, less, same).			
• letter identification.			
• finds a word that rhymes with _____.			
• find a word that begins like _____.			
• rereading message.			
• finding words the children know (familiar or interesting to them).			
• capital versus lowercase letters.			
The lesson lasts as long as the children.			

1. Not observed in lesson.
2. Evidence from observation suggests that teacher may need additional support and practice.
3. Evidence from observation suggests that teacher is implementing with understanding.

Comments _____

_____

_____

_____

_____

_____

_____

_____

_____

_____

_____

_____

_____

_____

_____

_____

_____

_____

Writing with Children Using Predictable Charts

What is writing with children using predictable charts?

Predictable charts are weekly sources of writing opportunities for the kindergarten classroom. Because they play such an important role in the development of readers and writers in a Building-Blocks classroom, there is a separate checklist for this writing activity. Teachers build word recognition and concepts of print by following this weekly format.

Why is it important?

By using predictable charts, which was once called "structured language experience," all students will be able to participate, regardless of their own language skills. Students see themselves as readers and writers. (Cunningham, 1979, Hall and Williams, 2000; Hall and Williams, 2001)

The following two-page list contains key elements of this important classroom activity. It is not an all-inclusive list but rather a guide for observation.

	1	2	3
Day One and Two—Sentence Dictation			
The sentence on the chart has a curricular tie (related to a book, field trip, holiday, etc.).			
The teacher models completing the predictable sentence by doing a sentence first.			
Students must state a complete sentence when giving their ending ("I would fly to Florida," not just "Florida.")			
The teacher models writing each sentence as the child dictates it.			
The child's name is placed in parentheses after his or her sentence.			
Each student contributes to the chart (may take two days).			
The lesson lasts as long as the children.			
Day Three—Touch Reading (Tracking Print)			
Each child "touch reads" his or her sentence on the chart.			
The teacher provides students with sentences on sentences strips to cut up on their own.*			
The teacher may write the words out of order on the sentence strip.*			
Each student arranges his or her cut-up sentence and "touch reads" it to a partner.*			
Students may arrange their partners' cut-up sentences.*			
Students "touch read" cut-up sentences to partners or the teacher.*			
The lesson lasts as long as the children.			
* Time permitting after making several predictable charts.			

The Administrator's Guide to Building Blocks™

	1	2	3

Day Four—Sentence Builders

	1	2	3
The teacher has prepared approximately three sentences from the chart before the lesson for the sentence builders activity.			
The teacher distributes the word cards randomly for one sentence.			
Students with word cards come to the front of the class and "build" the sentence.			
The class reads the built sentence together.			
Once the sentence is built, the teacher asks, "What do you notice?"			
The teacher then works on identifying words, finding words that begin with the same letter/sound, finding the longest and shortest word, clapping parts of words, finding words that rhyme, etc.			
The teacher repeats the sentence builder activity with two (or more) sentences.			
The lesson lasts as long as the children.			

Day Five—Making a Class Book

	1	2	3
The teacher distributes sentences on sentence strips to children in the class or each child copies his or her own sentence from the predictable chart.			
The students cut between the words on their own sentences.			
The children, sitting at tables or their desks, arrange the words in their sentences in the correct order. Some students may have to look at the predictable chart to be able to do this task.			
The teacher checks each child's sentence, and the child attaches his or her sentence to a page.			
Each child illustrates his or her own sentence page.			
The teacher assembles the pages into a class book. (This may take place after the lesson is over.)			
The lesson lasts as long as the children.			

1. Not observed in lesson.
2. Evidence from observation suggests that teacher may need additional support and practice.
3. Evidence from observation suggests that teacher is implementing with understanding.

Comments _____

_____

_____

_____

_____

_____

Interactive Writing with Children

What is interactive writing with children?

This activity provides an opportunity to share the pen between teacher and student. The teacher and class work together to decide on, and then to write the message. The writing is done interactively, allowing the student to write what he or she is capable of doing successfully.

Why is it important?

The teacher can provide even further assistance with listening for letter sounds, letter formation, and all print concepts. This activity does not begin until later in the year (about midyear) and can be used as frequently as students are ready to participate (headings for charts, Morning Message, classroom signs, etc.).

The following two-page list contains key elements of this important classroom activity. It is not an all-inclusive list but rather a guide for observation.

	1	2	3
The teacher, with or without student input, determines the message to be written.			
The teacher restates the sentence to be written.			
The pen is shared between the students and the teacher.			
The students write what they are capable of hearing and writing; the teacher completes necessary letters and words.			
All writing is written in standard form.			
The teacher corrects errors with "magic tape" or paper.			
The teacher and students stretch out words together.			
One or more students may help with a single piece of writing.			
The lesson lasts as long as the children.			

1. Not observed in lesson.
2. Evidence from observation suggests that teacher may need additional support and practice.
3. Evidence from observation suggests that teacher is implementing with understanding.

Comments _____

_____

_____

_____

_____

_____

The Administrator's Guide to Building Blocks™

	1	2	3
When constructing the text, the teacher may:			
• clap parts of words.			
• give clues for writing familiar words.			
• write all or part of any word or sentence.			
When revisiting the text for instruction, the teacher asks questions about:			
• letter identification.			
• capital vs. lowercase letters.			
• the numbers of letters in words.			
• the numbers of words in sentences.			
• words students know (are familiar/interesting to them).			
• the number of sentences.			
The lesson lasts as long as the students.			

1. Not observed in lesson.
2. Evidence from observation suggests that teacher may need additional support and practice.
3. Evidence from observation suggests that teacher is implementing with understanding.

Comments _____

_____

_____

_____

_____

_____

_____

_____

_____

_____

_____

_____

_____

_____

_____

_____

_____

_____

Children Writing by Themselves

What is children writing by themselves?

Children writing by themselves provides an opportunity for independent practice in writing. Students are allowed to write about topics of their choice. Daily time is allowed for students to write in a journal and/or in a Writing Center.

Why is it important?

Students write best about the things they know (Calkins, 1984, 1996; Graves, 1993). When students write about the things they know, they become deeply involved in their writing and are motivated (Calkins, 1996). Kindergarten students need opportunities to apply what they are learning about letters and sounds and aspects of writing learned when the teacher writes for and with students (Hall and Williams, 2000).

The following two-page list contains key elements of this important classroom activity. It is not an all-inclusive list but rather a guide for observation.

	1	2	3
The Writing Center is open every day.			
The teacher provides a variety of materials in the Writing Center: pencils, markers, crayons, a variety of paper, note cards, computer, etc.			
The teacher accepts all writing attempts.			
The children are allowed to copy words found around the room.			
The children are encouraged to "tell" about their stories.			
The teacher sets aside time for daily writing (20-30 minutes). This may be writing in a journal or writing on a piece of paper.			
During the writing mini-lessons, the teacher models the different ways kindergarten students can write (drawing, "driting," writing random letters, writing letters they hear in words, writing words they know, writing words they see in the room, writing sentences, etc.) or reminds some students of this if done previously.			
The teacher models the writing process in mini-lessons that last no more than five to seven minutes and focus on one specific skill or strategy.			
If the teacher has the technology to allow her to model writing on the computer he or she talks about where the space bar, punctuation keys, and shift key are located; how to make capital letters, etc.			

1. Not observed in lesson.
2. Evidence from observation suggests that teacher may need additional support and practice.
3. Evidence from observation suggests that teacher is implementing with understanding.

Comments _____

_____

	1	2	3
The teacher acts as a coach by:			
• conferencing to assist in topic choice.			
• assisting students in stretching out words.			
• making connections to mini-lessons, Morning Message, predictable charts, etc.			
• celebrating all writing attempts.			
• coaching when students write and use a keyboard.			
• coaching about use of writing conventions.			
The children are encouraged to stretch out words and use "phonics spelling."			
The children's writing is not edited by the teacher.			
The teacher provides opportunities for children to share their writing on a regular basis.			
The lesson lasts as long as the children.			

1. Not observed in lesson.
2. Evidence from observation suggests that teacher may need additional support and practice.
3. Evidence from observation suggests that teacher is implementing with understanding.

Comments _____

_____

_____

_____

_____

_____

_____

_____

_____

_____

_____

_____

_____

_____

_____

_____

_____

Phonemic Awareness

What is phonemic awareness?
Phonemic awareness refers to a student's ability to hear the parts of words, separate the parts, put them back together, and then change them to make new words (Adams, 1990; Yopp, 1992). This is developed orally, without print.

Why is it important?
Phonemic awareness has been shown to be an indicator of reading success. The more students play with words orally, the more successful they will be reading them (Snow, Burns, and Griffin, 1998).

The following two-page list contains key phonemic awareness activities. These activities should be seen in other reading and writing checklists, as phonemic awareness is best taught in the context of real reading and writing. One or more of the following, but not all, may be observed in a lesson. It is not an all-inclusive list but rather a guide for observation.

	1	2	3
The teacher reads and discusses with children literature that focuses on some play with the sounds of language, including rhyming books, alphabet books, finger plays, songs, and poetry.			
The children learn and recite nursery rhymes.			
The children play with the beginning sounds of words ("*Kangaroo* starts like *Kaitlin*. What else starts like *kangaroo* and *Kaitlin*?").			
The teacher uses tongue twisters to teach beginning sounds.			
The children play with rhyming words ("*Bat* and *cat* rhyme. Does *rat* rhyme with *bat* and *cat*?")			
The teacher uses the Morning Message to discuss words that begin with the same sounds or have the same rhyme in them.			

1. Not observed in lesson.
2. Evidence from observation suggests that teacher may need additional support and practice.
3. Evidence from observation suggests that teacher is implementing with understanding.

Comments _____

_____

_____

_____

_____

The Administrator's Guide to Building Blocks™

	1	2	3
The children "clap" words into separate syllables (one clap for each syllable: Joey = 2 syllables = 2 claps).			
The teacher encourages children to supply words that rhyme with other words ("What rhymes with *cat*?").			
The teacher segments words into their individual sounds ("*Cat* has three sounds: c - a - t.").			
The teacher blends segmented sounds into words ("C - a - t is the word *cat*.").			
The teacher plays and encourages word games ("A *chair* without a "ch" becomes *air*.").			

1. Not observed in lesson.
2. Evidence from observation suggests that teacher may need additional support and practice.
3. Evidence from observation suggests that teacher is implementing with understanding.

Comments _____

_____

_____

_____

_____

_____

_____

_____

_____

_____

_____

_____

_____

_____

_____

_____

_____

_____

_____

_____

Letters and Sounds

What is letters and sounds?
Letters and sounds refers to identifying the names and sounds of the letters of the alphabet.

Why is it important?
Children that can identify the names and sounds of the letters of the alphabet have a foundation that will help them as they later learn sight words and how to decode new words (Snow, Burns, and Griffin, 1998). A child's level of letter and sound learning is correlated to their reading success.

The following two-page list contains key letter and sound activities. These activities should be seen in other reading and writing checklists as letters and sounds are best taught in the context of real reading and writing. One or more of the following, but not all, may be observed in a lesson. It is not an all-inclusive list but rather a guide for observation.

	1	2	3
The teacher uses "Getting-to-Know-You" activities to provide the foundation for learning most letter names and sounds (The "j" sound is taught when *Jason* is the student of the day and is interviewed in the "Getting-to-Know-You" activities.).			
The teacher is sure to teach letters and sounds during real reading and writing activities (predictable charts, Morning Message, shared reading, and student writing). He or she does not use worksheets and workbooks.			
The teacher reads and discusses literature with the children that focuses on some play with the sounds of language (including rhyming books, alphabet books, and poetry).			
The teacher reads big books with students so that they can focus on words that begin alike.			
The teacher reads aloud alphabet books and makes them available for children to read.			
The teacher discusses beginning sounds of familiar words (days of the week, student names, etc.).			

1. Not observed in lesson.
2. Evidence from observation suggests that teacher may need additional support and practice.
3. Evidence from observation suggests that teacher is implementing with understanding.

Comments _____

_____

_____

_____

	1	2	3
The teacher writes the Morning Message with students so that letter names and sounds can be identified.			
The teacher prints tongue twisters so letter names and sounds can be discussed.			
The students are encouraged to use "phonics" spelling when they are writing.			
Students participate in Making Words lessons. They "become" a letter by wearing a letter card attached to a yarn necklace. A child with a beginning letter stands with a child wearing a familiar ending pattern to make words ("b" connects with "at" to become *bat*).			
The teacher finds rhyming words in books and writes them for children to see.			

1. Not observed in lesson.
2. Evidence from observation suggests that teacher may need additional support and practice.
3. Evidence from observation suggests that teacher is implementing with understanding.

Comments _____

_____

_____

_____

_____

_____

_____

_____

_____

_____

_____

_____

_____

_____

_____

_____

_____

_____

_____

Interesting Words

What is interesting words?

Interesting words for kindergarten students refers to some "interesting-to-them-words" like names, favorite restaurants, cereals, etc., that will later help them later as they learn other words that begin with the same letters and sounds.

Why is it important?

Children that can read some words store letter name and sound knowledge in the associative memory, making it easier for them to retrieve the information and use it in another learning situation.

The following list contains key activities for learning words. These activities should be seen in other reading and writing checklists as words are best taught in the context of real reading and writing. One or more of the following, but not all, may be observed in a lesson. It is not an all-inclusive list but rather a guide for observation.

	1	2	3
The teacher uses "Getting-to-Know-You" activities to introduce children to one another, to help teach letters and sounds, and to help students learn to identify the names of the other children in class.			
The teacher introduces capital and lowercase letters during "Getting to Know You" activities, Morning Message, and predictable charts.			
The teacher uses print, in the form of classroom labels, books, posters, and student work, throughout the room.			
The teacher uses environmental print (cereal boxes, restaurant bags and cups, road signs, and professional and collegiate sports team products) to introduce children to commonly seen words.			
The teacher displays developmentally appropriate Word Walls in the classroom. Later in the year (fourth quarter), some teachers may choose to display some high-frequency words in or near the Writing Center. It is important that words are only added after multiple exposures and experiences. This is different from the Word Wall and Word Wall activities seen in grades one through five.			

1. Not observed in lesson.
2. Evidence from observation suggests that teacher may need additional support and practice.
3. Evidence from observation suggests that teacher is implementing with understanding.

Comments _____

_____

_____

Later in the Year
A Glance at a Typical Week's Lesson
for
Reading

Monday

Today the teacher reads aloud the book *Is Your Mama a Llama?* by Deborah Guarino.

For shared reading, the class is beginning the big book *What Will the Weather Be Like Today?* by Paul Rogers. Students predict what they think the book will be about based on the cover and title. The teacher reads the big book to the class. After reading it, the teacher and class talk about their prediction and if they were right.

The children read their self-selected books for 8 to 10 minutes. Some children are really reading. Other children are reading the pictures or retelling the stories.

Tuesday

The story for the teacher read aloud today is *An Aardvark Flew an Airplane...and Other Silly Alphabet Rhymes* by David Dadson.

For shared reading, the teacher and the class review the different types of weather in *What Will the Weather Be Like Today?* The teacher reads the book again, stopping before some words and letting the children "read" the weather words. After reading, the teacher writes the weather words on sentence strips and illustrates each word. The children are given a paper folded into four boxes. They write and illustrate weather words: sunny, cloudy, windy, and rainy.

The children read their self-selected books for 8 to 10 minutes. Some children are really reading. Other children are reading the pictures or retelling the stories

Wednesday

The teacher reads aloud the book *How the Camel Got His Hump* by Rudyard Kipling.

The children talk about the book *What Will the Weather Be Like Today?* before they read it in an echo-reading format. After reading, the children compare what is in the book to the weather in their area.

The children read their self-selected books for 8 to 10 minutes. Some children are really reading. Other children are reading the pictures or retelling the stories.

Thursday

Today the teacher reads a rhyming story, *Peanut Butter and Jelly: A Play Rhyme* by Nadine Bernard Westcott.

The teacher and the class try to remember the weather in the book *What Will the Weather Be Like Today?* They try to arrange the sentences from the book that the teacher has written in the order the author wrote them. The teacher and the class reread the book with a choral reading. After reading, they discuss if the sequenced sentences are in the right order. If not, they will rearrange these sentences.

The children read their self-selected books for 8 to 10 minutes. Some children are really reading. Other children are reading the pictures or retelling the stories.

Friday

The book the teacher reads today is *Sheep in a Jeep* by Nancy Shaw.

The final reading of the big book *What Will the Weather Be Like Today?* will be done with some children acting out what they would do during certain types of weather. The class decides what to do on a sunny day, a cloudy day, a windy day, and a rainy day. The teacher and the class will do a choral reading with half the class reading the book and half the class "acting." This is repeated so everyone can read and everyone can "do the book." After the lesson, the teacher and students review what they learned or know about weather.

The children read their self-selected books for 8 to 10 minutes. Some children are really reading. Other children are reading the pictures or retelling the stories.

Later in the Year
A Glance at a Typical Week's Lessons
for
Writing

Monday

The teacher writes *for* children right after Big Group when she writes the Morning Message:

> Dear Class,
>   Today is Monday. It is windy outside.
>   It would be a great day to fly a kite.
> Love,
>   Mrs. Arens

The teacher writes *with* children using a predictable chart. It is the first day, so she begins by writing her sentence and half the children dictate their sentences for her to write:

> If I Were a Kite
> I would fly to Italy. (Mrs. Arens)
> I would fly to Chicago. (Alex)
> I would fly to Grandma's. (Jeff)
> I would fly to . . .

The Writing Center is open for children to write *by themselves*. The children also write by themselves in a journal at writing time.

Mini-lesson: (Writing for)

The teacher draws a kite and demonstrates how she can write about her kite. She is sure to stretch out words and models writing the letters she hears:

> My Kite
> My kite is red, wit, and blu. I will run
> with my kite. Up, up in the sky it will go. Flying
> kites is fun!

The teacher conferences with Alex, William, and Karen, and the same students share their writing at the end of writing time.

Tuesday

The first time the teacher writes *for* children is right after Big Group when she writes the Morning Message:

> Dear Class,
>   Today is Tuesday, March 12. We have a new
> student today. Her name is Sue. Be a good
> friend.
>   Love,
>   Mrs. Arens

The teacher writes *with* children and finishes the predictable chart they started yesterday:

> I would fly to Atlanta. (Merrill Kaye)
> I would fly to Maine. (Jeff)
> I would fly to New York. (Devon)
> I would fly to . . .

The Writing Center is open for children to write *by themselves*. The children also write by themselves in a journal at writing time.

The Administrator's Guide to Building Blocks™

Mini-lesson: (Writing for)

The teacher works some more on the kite story she started yesterday. She is sure to stretch out words and models writing the letters she hears:

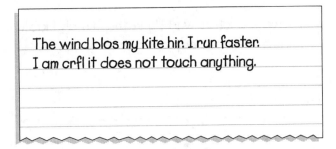

The wind blos my kite hir. I run faster.
I am crfl it does not touch anything.

The teacher conferences with Katie, Susie, Lafe, and Brad, and the same students share their writing at the end of writing time.

Wednesday

The teacher writes *for* children right after Big Group when she writes the Morning Message:

Dear Class,
   Today is Wednesday, March 13. All 13 days in March have been like a lion. When will we have a day like a lamb?
   Love,
   Mrs. Arens

The teacher wrote *with* children using a predictable chart on Monday and Tuesday. Today, all the children "touch read" their sentences. Then, they match their cut-up sentences to the sentences on the chart.

The class does some interactive writing as the children and the teacher write a chart for the science experiment: What will magnets pick up?

What will magnets pick up?

The Writing Center is open for children to write *by themselves*. The children also write by themselves in a journal at writing time.

Mini-lesson: (Writing for)

The teacher writes another story about a kite. She is sure to stretch out words and models writing the letters she hears:

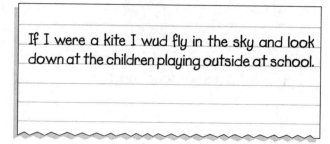

If I were a kite I wud fly in the sky and look down at the children playing outside at school.

The teacher conferences with Elinor, Janet, Patty, and Karen, and the same students share their writing at the end of writing time.

Thursday

The teacher writes *for* children twice today. The first time is right after Big Group when she writes the Morning Message for the children:

Dear Class,
    Today is Thursday, March 14. It looks like it will be a very nice day. We will take a walk around the neighborhood. What will we see?
    Love,
    Mrs. Arens

The teacher wrote *with* children using a predictable chart on Monday and Tuesday. Today, the children do Sentence Builders and build four sentences chosen by the teacher.

The class does some interactive writing as the children help write two sentences about their trip around the neighborhood for social studies:

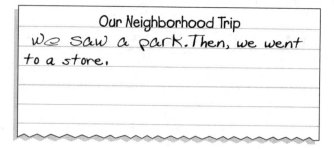

Our Neighborhood Trip
We saw a park. Then, we went to a store.

The Writing Center is open for children to write *by themselves*.

The teacher continues the kite story she started yesterday. She is sure to stretch out words and models writing the letters she hears:

> I wud look for my friends. I wud fly up over the school.

Rhonda, Victoria, John, and Erin will share their writing with the class.

Friday

The teacher writes *for* children twice today. The first time is right after Big Group when she writes the Morning Message for the children:

> Dear Class,
>   Today is Friday. I hope you have a great weekend. Be sure to read some books. Someone will get to take home our class book today.
>   Love,
>   Mrs. Arens

The teacher has written *with* the children using a predictable chart on Monday and Tuesday. Today, each child makes a page for the class book by pasting his or her sentence on a piece of paper and illustrating it.

The class does some interactive writing in math as the children and teacher make a shapes sign that will be placed in the Math Center. They write:

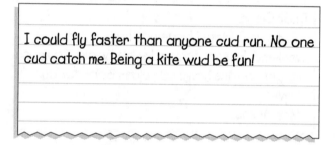

The Writing Center is open for children to write *by themselves.*

The teacher reads the kite story she has written. She continues writing, stretching out words and modeling writing the letters she hears:

I could fly faster than anyone cud run. No one cud catch me. Being a kite wud be fun!

Karen, Susie, Patty, and Dana will share their writing with the class.

Later in the Year
A Glance at a Typical Week's Lessons
for
Phonemic Awareness, Letters and Sounds,
and Interesting Words

Monday
Children watch as the teacher writes the Morning Message. They raise their hands to correct errors she makes. Today, she forgets to add a capital letter at the beginning of a sentence, and she leaves out the word *and*.

The children learn a new tongue twister: Mommy made me mush my marshmallows. They read it together several times. Then, they replace *mommy* with "M" names from the Name Wall (Megan, Matt, MacKenzie, etc.). When they have learned the tongue twister, they go to their seats and write tongue twisters. They can write the one from the chart, replace *mommy* with another "M" name, or they can make up their own. If students finish early they can illustrate their tongue twisters.

The teacher reads *Is Your Mama a Llama?* by Deborah Guarino. Children provide the rhyme during the second reading. The teacher writes the rhyme for the children to see.

Tuesday
Children sing "Teacher" (see page 34). They segment the first sound in the name of the animal (/c/ /c/ /c/ -at). When the verse is over, they shout the letter that makes that sound "C!"

Today is journal day. The teacher writes in her "journal" using the board. She writes about a movie she saw the night before. She segments the words she is unsure of, telling the children she will stretch out the words so she can hear all of the sounds. Children write in their journals when she is done. They may write about a favorite movie, something they did, or something they want to tell about. The teacher coaches the children as they write. She visits with Steve and Linda first. They sometimes need the most help getting started. When they are done, each child reads her entry to the class.

The story today is *An Aardvark Flew an Airplane...and Other Silly Alphabet Rhymes* by David Dadson.

Wednesday
The teacher writes the Morning Message as children watch. She tells them that today is "hump" day because it is in the middle of the week.

Then, she reads the book *How the Camel Got His Hump* by Rudyard Kipling. The children brainstorm other examples of animals and how they came to be (*How the Bee Got Her Buzz, How the Cat Got Her Purr, How the Lightning Bug Got His Light,* etc.). The ideas are written on chart paper and posted on the wall. The children may use these ideas for their journal writing, and they may choose to write a class book about one of these animals or bugs in the next few weeks.

Thursday

The children visit the Environmental Print Wall looking at the cereal boxes, restaurant logos, and sports team logos that they have brought in. They read and chant all of the team logos. Today, they add the Kansas City Chiefs. Adam's dad used to play for the Chiefs. He brings in a Chief's flag to go on the Environmental Print Wall. The children see that Chiefs, Cheerios®, Cheezits®, and Chips Ahoy® begin with the /ch/ sound.

The teacher then plays "Guess My Word" by saying the sounds in a word and children have to guess what the word is (/c/ /a/ /t/ = cat). After a few examples, children are invited to choose a picture card. They say the sounds of the picture, and the rest of the class tries to guess the word. When it is guessed correctly, they show the picture card.

Today's story is the rhyming book *Peanut Butter and Jelly: A Play Rhyme* by Nadine Bernard Westcott. Children read the story with the teacher during the second reading. They write a class book about making pepperoni pizza.

Friday

The children read the Morning Message as the teacher writes it. They read that they are going to make words today. The children cheer when they read this!

Today's book is the big book version of *Sheep in a Jeep* by Nancy Shaw. Children read along during the second reading. After that, the teacher writes the rhyming words on the board as the children identify rhyming words. She focuses their attention on the -eep words. Then, she gives one child a "yarn necklace" that has a card with "eep" written on it. She hands out other necklaces with "sh," "j," "w," "st," and "b" on them. The child with the "eep" card comes to the front of the room. She invites the child wearing "sh" to come up and stand beside the child wearing "eep." The teacher slowly says /sh/ then /eep/. She begins blending them together until the children say "sheep." They continue this until all five words are made. Then, she redistributes the letter necklaces. This time she allows the children in the audience to blend the sounds to make the words. Finally, she adds a new letter necklace with "k." She tells children this word wasn't in the story, but she is sure they can make this word. She has the children say the sounds to themselves, then they all say "keep" out loud.

Teacher's Planning Checklists
Later in the Year

A few words of caution about the use of the following pages...

The following checklists offered in this book are intended to convey the basics of the Building-Blocks™ model. The model is not rigidly defined, especially as teachers gain confidence in the delivery and begin to interject more of their own personalities and creativity. However, some elements define the model, provide the careful balance, are multilevel, and ensure a greater level of success. These checklists are offered in response to administrators and teachers who have asked for more specific details in an attempt to do a better job of getting the Building Blocks™ Model started.

Also, when the checklists mention that the lessons "last as long as the children," it is a reference to ending the lessons when the children are no longer engaged in learning.

Reading to Children

As I prepare and present lessons for reading to children later in the year, I am sure to . . .

_____ 1. Provide a good model of fluency in reading and attempt to motivate students through a daily teacher read-aloud. My read-aloud is clear, expressive, and enthusiastic.

_____ 2. Promote reading through teacher read-alouds and talk about books at one or several appropriate times throughout the day

_____ 3. Model the types of questions during closure time that will lead young students to think about and discuss the story.

_____ 4. Connect my read-alouds, when possible, to a subject, theme, or concept that the class has studied, is studying, or will study in the near future.

_____ 5. Connect the read-alouds, when possible, to my life, the students' lives, and/or the real world.

_____ 6. Make the lesson last as long as the children.

Reading with Children

As I prepare and present lessons for reading with children later in the year, I am sure to . . .

_____ 1. Choose a familiar nursery rhyme, song, poem, or big book predictable by pictures or print.

_____ 2. Provide activities or discussion before reading to prepare the children for what they will read (setting, characters, vocabulary, etc.).

_____ 3. Give the children a first reading which is clear, expressive, and enthusiastic.

_____ 4. Reread the story or selection several times using shared, echo, or choral reading with all children joining in.

_____ 5. Provide activities after reading to help the children understand what they read (talk about the story, sequence the events, "act it out," draw, "drite," etc.).

_____ 6. Work with high-frequency words or rhyming words used in the story (sentence builders, finding high-frequency words, finding rhyming words, etc.).

_____ 7. Help students become aware of letters and sounds (letter/sounds of some important words, words that start alike, etc.).

_____ 8. Compare the book or story to another book or story read previously.

_____ 9. Make a souvenir (art activity) to remember the story and as a retelling prompt.

_____ 10. Make the lesson last as long as the children.

Children Reading by Themselves

As I prepare and present lessons for children reading by themselves later in the year, I am sure to . . .

_____ 1. Provide an adequate supply of books and other reading materials on various topics, of different genres, and on varied reading levels appropriate for kindergarten students. I organize the materials in the Reading Center using tubs or crates which can be brought to the students' tables during self-selected reading time.

_____ 2. Make books easily accessible to children so that they will not lose time in choosing and changing books.

_____ 3. Check to see that I have had a conference with every child in the class in the last week; if not, I plan for it by dividing the class into days of the week.

_____ 5. Limit the time spent on each conference so I can spend time with several students.

_____ 6. Check to see that I "ooh" and "aah" over the books the children are reading as much or more than I ask questions.

_____ 7. During conferences, guide and encourage children who can read, to read books on the appropriate levels, while still allowing freedom of choice.

_____ 8. Let children choose how they want to read their books to me (read the words, read the pictures, or retell the story).

_____ 9. Make the lesson last as long as the children.

Writing for Children

As I prepare and present lessons in writing for children later in the year, I am sure to . . .

_____ 1.   Ask for input on what to write about.

_____ 2.   Talk or think aloud while I am writing.

_____ 3.   Write, and while I am writing I:

___ spell words aloud.

___ explain the use of punctuation.

___ describe the formation of letters.

___ reread the message as I write.

___ use one-to-one pointing as I read.

___ use terms such as _opening, closing, greeting, message, word, sentence, period, question mark, exclamation mark_, etc.

_____ 4.   Ask children who still need the experience to count the words in the sentences.

_____ 5.   Ask children who still need the experience to compare the number of words in the sentences.

_____ 6.   Ask children who still need the experience to count the number of letters in a sentence.

_____ 7.   Ask children who still need the experience to compare the numbers of letters in the sentences.

_____ 8.   Ask the students to tell me what they notice about the writing.

_____ 9.   Accept the responses the children give.

_____ 10.   Ask the children to find words they know.

_____ 11.   Make the lesson last as long as the children.

Writing with Children Using Predictable Charts

As I prepare and present five-day lessons for writing with children using predictable charts later in the year, I am sure to . . .

Day One and Two:

_____ 1.   Decide on a curricular tie-in for our class predictable chart.

_____ 2.   Begin by modeling my own sentence.

_____ 3.   Ask each student to say the complete sentence ("I would fly to Chicago.")

_____ 4.   Write each sentence in front of the class.

_____ 5.   Make the lesson last as long as the children.

Day Three:

_____ 1.   Prepare a sentence for each student. I may write the words out of order on some sentence strips.

_____ 2.   Model cutting between the words on the sentence strips.

_____ 3.   Observe as students cut their sentences between words.

_____ 4.   Observe as each child (at his or her seat or on the floor) matches his or her sentence with the text on the chart.

_____ 5.   Observe as each child "touch reads" his or her sentence to me or a partner.

_____ 6.   Observe as some students may arrange a partner's sentence, as well.

_____ 7.   Make the lesson last as long as the children.

Day Four:

_____ 1. Prepare word cards for at least three sentences.

_____ 2. Randomly distribute word cards for one sentence, giving one word per person.

_____ 3. Ask students to come forward and build the sentence, matching the text on the pocket chart.

_____ 4. Lead the students in reading the sentence as I touch the head of each child (word) in the sentence.

_____ 5. Ask questions such as:

    ___ "Can you find the word _like_?

    ___ "Can you find a word that begins like _Merrill_?"

    ___ "Can you find a word that rhymes with _will_?"

    ___ "Can you find the longest word?"

    ___ "Can you find the shortest word?"

    ___ "How many parts (syllables) does _Montgomery_ have?"

_____ 6. Repeat the process with two or more sentences, as long as the learners are ready.

_____ 7. Make the lesson last as long as the children.

Day Five:

_____ 1. Arrange my cut-up sentence on a large page and either draw or describe what I will draw to match my words. I demonstrate gluing the words in order on the page.

_____ 2. Provide each student with his or her cut-up sentence, or students are asked to copy sentences from a chart or strip.

_____ 3. Observe while students cut between the words on the strips and arrange their sentences on their pages.

_____ 4. Check for accuracy before the student glues down the words.

_____ 5. Observe as the children illustrate their pages.

_____ 6. Assemble the pages into a class book.

_____ 7. Make the lesson last as long as the children.

Interactive Writing with Children

As I prepare and present lessons in writing with children later in the year, I am sure to . . .

_____ 1.   Make the decisions or ask for input on what to write about.

_____ 2.   Talk or think aloud while I am writing.

_____ 3.   Restate the sentence we are about to write.

_____ 4.   Share the responsibility of the pen with the students when I know they can be successful.

_____ 5.   Check that all writing is correctly spelled, capitalized, and punctuated, or is corrected with "magic tape."

_____ 6.   Help the students stretch out words.

7.   While writing I:

___ spell words aloud.

___ explain the use of punctuation.

___ describe the formation of letters.

___ reread the message as I write.

___ use one-to-one pointing as I read.

_____ 8.   Once the writing is complete, I ask the students to tell me what they notice.

9.   Possible ideas for instruction include:

___ identifying letters   ___ matching capitals and lowercase letters

___ finding familiar words   ___ using ending punctuation

___ finding rhyming words   ___ counting words or letters in sentences

_____ 10.   Make the lesson last as long as the children.

The Administrator's Guide to Building Blocks™

Children Writing by Themselves

As I prepare and present lessons in writing with children early in the year, I am sure to . . .

_____ 1.   Model for my students the different ways they can write in kindergarten (drawing, "driting," writing letters, writing words, writing sentences).

_____ 2.   Think aloud as I write my mini-lesson.

_____ 3.   Verbalize what I am doing and why as I write my mini-lesson.

_____ 4.   Find words around the room that I can copy. I also stretch out words and write the sounds I hear, writing one or two words in their "phonics" or sound spelling as a model for children.

_____ 5.   Model how to choose a topic.

_____ 6.   Model how to return to a piece of writing and add to it.

_____ 7.   Coach my students when they are ready to write.

_____ 8.   Not spell for my students but let them do the work.

_____ 9.   Allow my students to compose on the computer (if one is available).

_____ 10.   Provide opportunities for my students to share their writing.

_____ 11.   Make the lesson last as long as the children.

The Administrator's Guide to Building Blocks™

Phonemic Awareness

In preparing and presenting lessons in phonemic awareness later in the year, I am sure to . . .

_____ 1. Use literature that focuses on some play with the sounds of language, including rhyming books, alphabet books, and poetry.

_____ 2. Read and discuss books, songs, or poems with children.

_____ 3. Have children read, learn, and recite nursery rhymes.

_____ 4. Have children play with the beginning sounds of words (_"Kangaroo_ starts like _Kaitlin_. What else starts like _kangaroo_ and _Kaitlin_?"_).

_____ 5. Use tongue twisters to teach beginning sounds.

_____ 6. Have children play with rhyming words (_"Bat_ and _cat_ rhyme. Does _rat_ rhyme with _bat_ and _cat_?"_).

_____ 7. Use the Morning Message to discuss words that begin with the same sounds or rhyme.

_____ 8. Have children "clap" words into separate syllables (one clap for each syllable: Joey = 2 syllables = 2 claps).

_____ 9. Encourage children to supply words that rhyme with other words ("What rhymes with _cat_?").

_____ 10. Have children segment words into their individual sounds ("Cat has three sounds: /c/ /a/ /t/.").

_____ 11. Have children blend segmented sounds into words ("/C/ /a/ /t/ is the word _cat_.").

_____ 12. Have children play word games ("A _chair_ without /ch/ becomes _air_.").

Letters and Sounds

In preparing and presenting lessons to teach letters and sounds later in the year, I am sure to . . .

_____ 1. Use "Getting-to-Know-You" activities to provide the foundation for learning most letter names and sounds (The "j" sound is taught when *Jason* is the student of the day and is interviewed in the "Getting-to-Know-You" activities.).

_____ 2. Teach letters and sounds during real reading and writing activities (predictable charts, Morning Message, shared reading, and student writing). Worksheets and workbooks are not used.

_____ 3. Read and discuss literature that focuses on some play with the sounds of language, including rhyming books, alphabet books, and poetry.

_____ 4. Read big books with students so that words that begin alike can be focused on.

_____ 5. Read alphabet books to children and make them available for children to read.

_____ 6. Discuss the beginning sounds of familiar words (days of the week, student names, etc.).

_____ 7. Write the Morning Message with students so that letter names and sounds can be identified. I let the students tell me what letters to write and share the pen with children who can write the beginning sound of words.

_____ 8. Print tongue twisters so letter names can be discussed along with letter sounds.

_____ 9. Encourage children to use "phonics" spelling when they are writing.

_____ 10. Have students participate in Making Words lessons. They "become" a letter by wearing a letter card attached to a yarn necklace. A child with a beginning letter stands with a child wearing a familiar ending pattern to make words ("b" connects with "at" to become *bat*).

_____ 11. Find and write rhyming words for children to see.

Interesting Words

In preparing and presenting lessons for interesting words later in the year, I am sure to . . .

_____ 1. Use "Getting-to-Know-You" activities to introduce children to one another, to learn letters and sounds, and to learn to identify the names of the other children in class.

_____ 2. Introduce capital and lowercase letters during "Getting-to-Know-You" activities.

_____ 3. Display print, in the form of classroom labels, books, posters, and student work, throughout the room.

_____ 4. Display environmental print (cereal boxes, restaurant logos, road signs, professional and collegiate sports teams products, etc.) to introduce children to commonly seen words.

_____ 5. Display developmentally appropriate Word Walls in the classroom. Later in the year (fourth quarter), some teachers may choose to display some high-frequency words in or near the Writing Center. It is important that words are only added after multiple exposures and experiences. This is different from the Word Wall and Word Wall activities seen in grades one through five.

Professional References

Adams, M. J. (1990) *Beginning to Read: Learning and Thinking about Print*. Cambridge, MA: MIT Press.

Anderson, R. C., Hiebert, E. H., Scott, J. A., and Wilkinson, I. A. G. (1984) *Becoming a Nation of Readers: The Report of the Commission on Reading*. Washington, DC: U. S. Department of Education.

Calkins, L. (1986, 1996) *The Art of Teaching Writing*. Portsmouth, NH: Heinemann.

Cunningham, P. M. (2000) *Phonics They Use, 3rd Edition*. New York: Addison-Wesley Publishing Co.

Cunningham, P. M. "Beginning Reading without Readiness: Structured Language Experience." *Reading Horizons* (Spring 1979) 222-227.

Cunningham, P. M. and Allington, R. L. (1998) *Classrooms that Work, 2nd. Edition*. New York: Addison-Wesley Publishing Co..

Cunningham, P. M. and Allington, R. L. (2002) *Classrooms that Work, 3rd. Edition*. New York: Addison-Wesley Publishing Co..

Cunningham, P. M. and Hall, D. P. (1996) *Building Blocks: A Framework for Reading and Writing in Kindergartens that Work*. (Video) Clemmons, NC: Windward Productions.

Cunningham, P. M., Hall, D. P., and Defee, M. "Non-Ability Grouped, Multilevel Instruction: A Year in a First Grade Classroom." *The Reading Teacher, No. 44, 566-571*, 1991.

Cunningham, P. M., Hall, D. P., and Defee, M. "Non-Ability Grouped, Multilevel Instruction: Eight Years Later." *The Reading Teacher, No. 51*, 652-664, 1998.

Cunningham, P. M., Hall, D. P., and Gambrell, L. B. *Self-Selected Reading: The Four-Blocks® Way*. Greensboro, NC: Carson-Dellosa Publishing.

Gentry, J. R., "You Can Analyze Development Spelling—And Here's How to Do It!" *Early Years, K-8*, May, 192-200, 1985.

Gentry, J. R. and Gillet, J. W. (1993) *Teaching Kids to Spell*. Portsmouth, NH: Heinemann.

Graves, D. H. (1994) *A Fresh Look at Writing*. Portsmouth, NH: Heinemann.

Hall, D. P. and Cunningham, P. M. (1997) *Month-by-Month Reading and Writing for Kindergarten*. Greensboro, NC: Carson-Dellosa Publishing.

Hall, D. P. and Williams, E. (2000) *The Teacher's Guide to Building Blocks™*. Greensboro, NC: Carson-Dellosa Publishing.

Hall, D. P. and Williams, E. (2001) *Predictable Charts: Shared Writing for Kindergarten and First Grade*. Greensboro, NC: Carson-Dellosa Publishing.

Snow, C. E., Burns, M. S., and Griffin, P. Editors (1998) *Preventing Difficulties in Reading*. Washington, DC: National Academy Press.

Yopp, H. K. "Developing Phonemic Awareness" *The Reading Teacher, No. 45, 696-703*, 1992.

Children's Works Cited

An Aardvark Flew an Airplane…and Other Silly Alphabet Rhymes by David Dadsen (Little Thinker Books, 2000).

The Alphabet Tree by Leo Lionni (Knopf, 1990).

Brown Bear, Brown Bear, What Do You See? by Bill Martin (Harcourt Brace, 1993).

Color Zoo by Lois Ehlert (HarperCollins Publishers, 1997).

Frederick by Leo Lionni (Knopf, 1987).

How the Camel Got His Hump by Rudyard Kipling (North South Books, 2001).

I Went Walking by Susan Williams (Harcourt, 1992).

Is Your Mama a Llama? by Deborah Guarino (Scholastic, 1989).

Miss Mary Mack: A Hand-Clapping Rhyme by Mary Ann Hoberman (Little Brown & Co., 1998).

Peanut Butter and Jelly: A Play Rhyme by Nadine Bernard Wescott (Houghton Mifflin, 1991).

Read Aloud Rhymes for the Very Young by Jack Prelutsky (Knopf, 1986).

Sheep in a Jeep by Nancy Shaw (Houghton Mifflin, 1988).

What Will the Weather Be Like Today? by Paul Rogers (Scholastic, 1989).

The Z Was Zapped: A Play in Twenty-Six Acts by Chris Van Allsburg (Houghton Mifflin, 1987).

Zoo Looking by Mem Fox (Mondo, 1996).